What Motivates
Suicide Bombers?

Other books in the At Issue series:

What Motivates Suicide Bombers?

Lauri S. Friedman, *Book Editor*

Bruce Glassman, *Vice President*
Bonnie Szumski, *Publisher*
Helen Cothran, *Managing Editor*

GREENHAVEN PRESS
An imprint of Thomson Gale, a part of The Thomson Corporation

Detroit • New York • San Francisco • San Diego • New Haven, Conn.
Waterville, Maine • London • Munich

For more information, contact
Greenhaven Press
27500 Drake Rd.
Farmington Hills, MI 48331-3535
Or you can visit our Internet site at http://www.gale.com

LIBRARY OF CONGRESS CATALOGING-IN-PUBLICATION DATA
What motivates suicide bombers? / Lauri S. Friedman, book editor.
p. cm. — (At issue)
Includes bibliographical references and index.
ISBN 0-7377-2320-3 (lib. : alk. paper) — ISBN 0-7377-2321-1 (pbk. : alk. paper)
1. Terrorism. 2. Suicide bombers. 3. Martyrdom—Islam. I. Friedman, Lauri S. II. At issue (San Diego, Calif.)
HV6431.W475 2005
303.6'25—dc22   2004052315

Printed in the United States of America

Contents

Introduction

The terrorist attacks of September 11, 2001, inaugurated America into a world that had long existed for people of other nations: the mystifying and horrifying world of suicide terrorism. Since those attacks, in which nineteen Middle Eastern men hijacked four commercial aircraft and flew them into the World Trade Center towers and the Pentagon, the use of suicide bombers as weapons has escalated around the globe at alarming rates. For most Americans, it is inconceivable that people could intentionally kill themselves expressly to ensure the murder of others. Indeed, the attacks left Americans deeply confused about what motivated the perpetrators to commit these acts. Understandably, much of the focus after the attacks was on the men themselves, their histories and psychologies. However, such analyses ignore the fact that suicide bombers rarely plan and execute attacks on their own.

Suicide attacks are often called "senseless" by horrified observers, or described in media reports as "mindless terror." Yet despite the seeming irrationality of suicide bombers, their deadly acts are actually shrewd and calculating. Instead of being random and lone expressions of desperation, most acts of suicide terrorism are strategic acts of warfare, thoroughly planned and premeditated as any battlefield attack. As professor Arial Merari explains, "Suicide bombers don't strap on explosive backpacks in fits of divine revelation. Most attacks are arranged by organizations pursuing political agendas." Indeed, far from being spontaneous acts of rage or zeal, suicide attacks tend to be carefully plotted, and suicide bombers themselves undergo a careful screening process. In fact, terrorist organizations frequently turn would-be suicide bombers away if they don't meet certain requirements, such as a certain minimum age. The Palestinian terrorist group Islamic Jihad, for example, reportedly does not accept suicide bombers whose family members have been recently killed by the Israeli army. The group believes that such a person might be too emotional to successfully breach security checkpoints in order to get inside Israel where the attack is meant to take place. Suicide bombers are therefore thoroughly screened to make sure they can maintain a calm and self-disciplined demeanor even up to the minute they pull the cord on their explosive belts.

Sometimes suicide bombers rely on a team of associates who help them in various ways to arrive at their final destination. Not every member of a terrorist organization actually carries out suicide attacks; some are in charge of support duties, such as driving bombers to their intended destination or providing them with money or clothing needed to carry out their mission. One such member of a terrorist group, for example, was in charge of procuring a guitar for a suicide bomber, to complete her disguise as a traveling musician. Such an exacting process has led author David Brooks to call suicide bombing a "highly communitarian enterprise. . . . In not one instance has a lone, crazed Palestinian gotten hold of a bomb and gone off to kill Israelis. Suicide bombings are initiated by tightly run organizations that recruit, indoctrinate, train, and reward the bombers. These organizations do not seek depressed or mentally unstable people for their missions."

Suicide attacks are undertaken by men, women, and children ready to die for a cause they believe is just, such as liberating or defending their homeland. Therefore, suicide bombers often see themselves as patriotic warriors, not much different from troops elsewhere in the world. "A curious journalist once asked me," writes Palestinian sociologist Eyad Sarraj, "to introduce him to a potential martyr [suicide terrorist]. When the journalist asked, 'Why would you do it?' he was told, 'Would you fight for your country or not? Of course you would. You would be respected in your country as a brave man, and I would be remembered as a martyr.'"

In asking what motivates suicide bombers, many terrorism experts claim that it is important to recognize that, like other soldiers, suicide bombers are following orders, participating in a warfare campaign intended to overwhelm an enemy and rack up military victories. When combating suicide terrorism, therefore, it is perhaps more important to focus on those who instruct the terrorists to die rather than on the actual suicide bombers themselves. These people oversee attack after attack and expend enormous energy enticing new recruits to the fray. Ultimate culpability for suicide attacks therefore lies with them, many experts contend, and it is these leaders that must be targeted if suicide bombers are to be stopped. Abu Saber M.G., the father of a Palestinian who carried out a suicide attack in an Israeli city, wrote a letter to the editor of the London Arabic-language daily *Al-Hayat* in which he forcefully condemned those who coerce young people to become suicide bombers. Saber wrote:

> I ask, on my behalf and on behalf of every father and mother informed that their son has blown himself up: "By what right do these leaders [of Hamas and Islamic Jihad] send the young people, even young boys in the flower of their youth, to their deaths?" Who gave them religious or any other legitimacy to tempt our children and urge them to their deaths? . . . Why doesn't a single one of the leaders who cannot restrain himself in expressing his joy and ecstasy . . . every time a young Palestinian man or woman sets out to blow himself or herself up send his son?

Impassioned by their cause and emboldened by their leaders, suicide bombers are unswerving in their dedication to the thorough destruction of their enemies. Understanding what motivates them is critical to preventing suicide terrorism from becoming an even more popular tool of armies around the world. When considering the many factors that influence a suicide bomber to act, it is vital to remember the organization—its leaders and supporting players—who make the attack possible. After all, those who piloted the planes in the September 11 attacks are dead, but the organization behind them—al Qaeda—continues to operate.

1

Islam Advocates Suicide Terrorism

Peter David

Peter David is political editor of the Economist *magazine.*

It is difficult to divorce Islam from terrorism, especially when terrorists themselves say they are acting in the name of Islam. Indeed, modern Islamic thought actively advocates holy war against the United States and its allies. This thought has gained popularity across the Muslim world, resulting in suicide bombers and other terrorists. The perpetrators of the September 11, 2001, attacks on the United States cited Islam as the inspiration for their attack. Islam has thus clearly been a factor in motivating terrorists to carry out attacks against their perceived enemies.

M any Muslims do not like the label "Islamic terrorism" attached to the mass murders perpetrated by Osama bin Laden and his al-Qaeda organisation. Islam, they say, is a religion of peace, at peace, which has no more connection to the terrorism of Mr bin Laden than Christianity had to the 1970s terrorism of, say, the Baader-Meinhof gang in Germany or the Red Brigades in Italy.[1] Just call it terrorism, they say: keep Islam out of it.

That is not quite possible. When people are trying to kill you, especially when they are good at it, it is prudent to listen to the reasons they give. And Mr bin Laden launched his "war" explicitly in Islam's name. Indeed, three years before the twin

1. These were two terrorist groups that just happened to have Christian members but were not acting upon any Christian belief.

towers [collapsed in the terrorist attacks of September 11, 2001], he went to the trouble of issuing a lengthy "Declaration of the World Islamic Front for Jihad [holy war] against the Jews and the Crusaders", stating that "to kill Americans and their allies, both civil and military, is the individual duty of every Muslim who is able, until the Aqsa mosque [in Jerusalem] and the Haram mosque [in Mecca] are freed from their grip, and until their armies, shattered and broken-winged, depart from all the lands of Islam."

It may be objected that any bunch of psychopaths bent on mayhem is free to say whatever it likes about its motives. Just because al-Qaeda's people kill in the name of Islam does not mean that conflict with the West is an essential part of the faith. A Marxist terrorist may say that he is killing for the sake of the working class, and that he possesses a whole body of theory to justify this activity, and that this theory is subscribed to by many people. Does that mean that it is somehow in the essence of the working class to wage war on capitalism? No. But it does suggest that societies trying to deal with Marxist terrorism need to look at Marxist ideas, and gauge the extent to which they are believed.

By the same token, the problem for those who want to believe that Islam has nothing to do with Islamic terrorism is not only that the terrorists themselves say otherwise. It is also the existence of a whole body of theory that is called upon to justify this activity, and which has zealous adherents. Admittedly, much of this theory is modern, as political as it is religious, with origins in the late 20th century. It is described variously as "fundamentalism", "Islamism" or "political Islam" (though these terms and definitions will need closer inspection later). But some of it also has, or claims to have, connections with some of the fundamental ideas and practices of the religion itself.

Twentieth-century Islamic thought

A good place to start to understand the theory is with the ideas of Sayyid Qutb, a literary critic in the 1930s and 1940s and later an activist in Egypt's Muslim Brotherhood [a militant Islamic group] before being executed in 1966. In the late 1940s, Qutb spent two years living in America, an experience he hated and which appears to have turned him against what most people in the West would call modernity but which he saw as something much worse.

On returning to Egypt, Qutb wrote a series of books, many from prison, denouncing *jahiliyya* (ignorance), a state of affairs he categorised as the domination of man over man, or rather subservience to man rather than to Allah. Such a state of affairs, he said, had existed in the past, existed in the present and threatened to continue in the future. It was the sworn enemy of Islam. "In any time and place human beings face that clear-cut choice: either to observe the law of Allah in its entirety, or to apply laws laid down by man of one sort or another. That is the choice: Islam or *jahiliyya*. Modern-style *jahiliyya* in the industrialised societies of Europe and America is essentially similar to the old-time *jahiliyya* in pagan and nomadic Arabia. For in both systems, man is under the dominion of man rather than Allah."

> *When people are trying to kill you, especially when they are good at it, it is prudent to listen to the reasons they give.*

Qutb was not the first Muslim intellectual to look at the world this way. . . . But it is Qutb's story that offers the more interesting insight into the way Islamic terrorists think today.

One reason is that Qutb is a link with the present. The Muslim Brothers continue to operate in Egypt and elsewhere. Mr bin Laden and his deputy, Ayman al-Zawahiri, are former Brothers. More than this, the forces that Qutb believed to be undermining Islam in the 1950s and 1960s—capitalism, individualism, promiscuity, decadence—are still seen as potent threats (more potent, with "globalisation") by Muslims today.

Qutb lost faith in the pan-Arab nationalism that was the prevailing ideology of the Arab world in his own time. In a letter from prison he said that the homeland a Muslim should cherish was not a piece of land but the whole *Dar al-Islam* (Abode of Islam). Any land that hampered the practice of Islam or failed to apply [Islamic] *sharia* law "becomes ipso facto part of *Dar al-Harb* (the Abode of War). It should be combated even if one's own kith and kin, national group, capital and commerce are to be found there."

A straight line connects Qutb's letter from prison to the ideas of Mr bin Laden and his followers in al-Qaeda. Like Qutb, al-Qaeda's followers perceive Islam to be under a double attack:

not just military attack from a hostile West (in Iraq, Palestine, Chechnya and so forth) but also from within, where western values spread by impious regimes are undermining what it means to be a Muslim. This double attack, in the al-Qaeda world view, is to be resisted by *jihad* in both of the two meanings this notion has in Islam: personal striving for a more perfect submission to the faith, and armed struggle against Islam's enemies. These enemies include both the far enemy (America, Israel) and the near enemy (the impious or even apostate regimes of the Muslim world). For Mr bin Laden, the Saudi regime is now as much his enemy as is the United States.

A mixed response to Islamic terrorism among Muslims

How representative are such views? Around one in four of the people in the world are Muslims. Only a small fraction of these 1.5 billion Muslims will have heard of, let alone subscribe to, the ideas of theorists such as Qutb. No more than a few thousand people are involved in the violent activities of al-Qaeda and like-minded *jihadi* organisations. After September 11th, moreover, Muslim clerics and intellectuals joined ordinary Muslims throughout the world in denouncing the atrocity al-Qaeda had perpetrated in their name. By no means all of these were "moderates". One was Sheikh Fadlallah, the Beirut [Lebanon]-based ayatollah [Muslim cleric] often described as the spiritual guide of Hizbullah, the Iranian-inspired [terrorist group known as the] "party of God." He issued a *fatwa* [an Islamic edict] condemning the attack. Another condemnation came from Yusuf Qaradawi, a Qatar-based Egyptian television cleric with some fiery views and a following of millions.

> *The problem for those who want to believe that Islam has nothing to do with Islamic terrorism is . . . that the terrorists themselves say otherwise.*

All that is heartening. The trouble is that small groups can produce big consequences. Only 19 young men took part in the attacks of September 11th. But the 19 changed history.

Their action led within two years to an American-led invasion and military occupation of two Muslim countries, Afghanistan and Iraq. This in turn has damaged Muslim perceptions of the United States, and perhaps by extension of the West at large.

> *Small groups can produce big consequences. Only 19 young men took part in the attacks of September 11th. But the 19 changed history.*

A survey . . . by the Pew Global Attitudes Project reported that negative views of America among Muslims had spread beyond the Middle East to Indonesia—the world's most populous Muslim country—and Nigeria. In many Muslim states a majority thought that America might become a military threat to their own country. Solid majorities of Palestinians and Indonesians—and nearly half of those in Morocco and Pakistan—said they had at least some confidence in Osama bin Laden to "do the right thing regarding world affairs". Seven out of ten Palestinians said they had confidence in Mr bin Laden in this regard. . . .

Islam's connection to terrorism

Where does all this leave the relationship between Islam and Islamic terrorism? For the average Muslim Islam is merely a religion, a way of organising life in accordance with God's will. Is it a religion of peace or of violence? Like other religions, it possesses holy texts that can be invoked to support either, depending on the circumstances. Like the Bible, the Koran (which differs from the Bible in that Muslims take all of it to be the word of God dictated directly to Muhammad, his prophet) and the *hadith* [traditional stories about the prophet Muhammad] contain injunctions both fiery and pacific. Muslims are enjoined to show charity and compassion. Yes, Islam has a concept of *jihad* (holy war), which some Muslims think should be added to the five more familiar pillars of faith: the oath of belief, prayer, charity, fasting and pilgrimage. But the Koran also insists that there should be no compulsion in religion.

Islam and Christendom have clashed for centuries. But if there is something in the essence of Islam that predisposes its adherents to violent conflict with the West, it is hard to say what it might be. The search for the something might anyway be an exercise in futility, given that the essentials of the faith are so hotly contested. Islam has no pope or equivalent central authority (though some Shias aspire to one). This means, as Oxford University's James Piscatori has argued, that the religious authorities and the official *ulema* [the community of Islamic scholars] find themselves in competition with unofficial or popular religious leaders and preachers, Sufi [Islamic spiritual] movements, Islamist groups and lay intellectuals. "All of these and others claim direct access to scripture, purport to interpret its contemporary meaning, and thus effectively question whether any one individual or group has a monopoly on the sacred—even as they appropriate that right for themselves.". . .

It can seem as if the world inhabited largely by Muslims has now come into conflict with the world inhabited largely by non-Muslims. Islam the faith is not the answer to this question. But the history, sociology and politics of Islam are undoubtedly part of it.

2

Islam Does Not Advocate Suicide Terrorism

George W. Bush

George W. Bush is the forty-third president of the United States.

Islam is a peaceful religion that does not in any way condone terrorism. The suicide bombers who perpetrated the terrorist attacks of September 11, 2001, were not acting in accordance with Islam; indeed, they violated the basic tenets of Islam by murdering innocent people. The Muslims of America are outraged and saddened by the terrorist attacks perpetrated in their religion's name. All Americans must remember that terrorism and Islam have nothing in common, and Muslims must not be scapegoated for the September 11 attacks.

Editor's Note: The following remarks were addressed to leaders of the American Muslim community at the Islamic Center of Washington, D.C., on September 17, 2001.

Thank you all very much for your hospitality. We've just had a wide-ranging discussion on the matter at hand. Like the good folks standing with me, the American people were appalled and outraged at [the terrorist attacks of September 11, 2001]. And so were Muslims all across the world. Both Americans and Muslim friends and citizens, tax-paying citizens, and Muslims in [other] nations were just appalled and could not be-

George W. Bush, address at the Islamic Center of Washington, DC, September 17, 2001.

16

lieve what we saw on our TV screens [that showed hijacked planes crashing into the World Trade Center and the Pentagon].

These acts of violence against innocents violate the fundamental tenets of the Islamic faith. And it's important for my fellow Americans to understand that.

The English translation is not as eloquent as the original Arabic, but let me quote from the Koran, itself: "In the long run, evil in the extreme will be the end of those who do evil. For that they rejected the signs of Allah and held them up to ridicule."

The face of terror is not the true faith of Islam. That's not what Islam is all about. Islam is peace. These terrorists don't represent peace. They represent evil and war.

Islam is a peaceful religion

When we think of Islam we think of a faith that brings comfort to a billion people around the world. Billions of people find comfort and solace and peace. And that's made brothers and sisters out of every race—out of every race.

America counts millions of Muslims amongst our citizens, and Muslims make an incredibly valuable contribution to our country. Muslims are doctors, lawyers, law professors, members of the military, entrepreneurs, shopkeepers, moms and dads. And they need to be treated with respect. In our anger and emotion, our fellow Americans must treat each other with respect.

> *These acts of violence against innocents violate the fundamental tenets of the Islamic faith.*

Women who cover their heads [that is, wear a veil over their hair in accordance with Islamic law] in this country must feel comfortable going outside their homes. Moms who wear cover must be not intimidated in America. That's not the America I know. That's not the America I value.

I've been told that some fear to leave; some don't want to go shopping for their families; some don't want to go about their ordinary daily routines because, by wearing cover, they're afraid they'll be intimidated. That should not and that will not stand in America.

Those who feel like they can intimidate our fellow citizens to take out their anger don't represent the best of America, they represent the worst of humankind, and they should be ashamed of that kind of behavior.

This is a great country. It's a great country because we share the same values of respect and dignity and human worth. And it is my honor to be meeting with leaders who feel just the same way I do. They're outraged, they're sad. They love America just as much as I do.

I want to thank you all for giving me a chance to come by. And may God bless us all.

3

Despair and Hopelessness Motivate Suicide Bombers

Ilene R. Prusher

Ilene R. Prusher is a staff writer for the Christian Science Monitor.

Suicide bombings are a product of despair and hopelessness amid the Palestinian population. The Israeli occupation humiliates Palestinians, who live in an increasingly violent and lawless society. Moreover, most Palestinians have had to cope with the loss of a family member or friend who was killed by the Israeli army. Feeling bitter about their world, younger and younger Palestinians turn to suicide bombing as the only way to express their despair.

Sixteen-year-old Iyad Masri started to withdraw from everyone. He read loudly from the Koran [the Muslim holy book] until well after midnight, and blasted tapes of Koranic verses from behind his bedroom door.

His parents knew he was distraught over his younger brother's death two months ago. But they never imagined that Iyad would consider strapping a belt of explosives around his waist. In early January [2004], he met with members of Islamic Jihad, a Palestinian militant group that rejects all compromise with Israel. He asked them to prepare him to be a martyr, a suicide bomber. Iyad died days later when the belt went off accidentally, killing only himself.

The Masri family's tragedy is part of a trend that many Palestinians see as a worrisome mark of desperation: younger and younger Palestinians enlisting for suicide missions against Israel.

[In March 2004], a group of Palestinian boys—ages 12, 13, and 15—were caught trying to sneak into Israel with plans to gun down Israelis in the coastal town of Afula. They left behind a note telling their families to celebrate their martyrdom if they didn't make it home. The Israeli military says the boys were re-cruited by the Islamic Jihad and the [terrorist group] al-Aqsa Martyr's Brigades.

> *In a poll [taken in summer 2003], 36 percent of 12-year-old boys in Gaza said they believed that the best thing in life was to die as a martyr.*

"It's easier to convince the young ones to be suicide bombers," says Mrs. Masri, a thin, drawn woman who, until late January, was a mother of five. "They wash their brains, telling them about going to Paradise. These organizations in-cite them to be suicide bombers, and teenagers aren't able to make such decisions."

"Hope is diminishing"

Children here have increasingly grown to idolize suicide bombers and others who are seen as having sacrificed their lives for the Palestinian cause, says Dr. Eyad Serraj, a psychia-trist in the Gaza Strip. The reason, he says, is that they see "martyrdom" as the ultimate redemption. In a poll [taken in summer 2003], 36 percent of 12-year-old boys in Gaza said they believed that the best thing in life was to die as a martyr, ac-cording to Dr. Serraj.

"In their minds, the only model of power and glory is the martyr," he says. "Palestinian society glorifies the martyr. They are elevated to the level of saints and even prophets. Out of the hopeless and the inhuman environment they live in, there is the promise that they will have a better life in heaven."

The martyr's image . . . contrasts sharply with the way Palestinian youth view their fathers, Serraj says. In studies he's conducted, fathers are seen as "helpless, unable to protect his children in the face of [Israeli incursions]."

Palestinian leader Yasser Arafat is seen as an equally power-less figure, he adds. "There is a very big pool of potential mar-tyrs. They are queuing," he says, "and that happens because hope is diminishing."

"I tried to give him some hope"

For many young Palestinians, analysts note, the normal pres-sures of growing up are compounded by a mix of problems, personal and political. The past 3½ years of intifada [uprising] have brought a steady stream of violence between Israelis and Palestinians, as well as a growing sense of lawlessness as Mr. Arafat's Palestinian Authority continues to lose control over the West Bank and Gaza Strip.

Iyad's parents say that his frustration grew with a long pe-riod of school closures here, and he refused to return to school last year [2003]. He decided to work in construction instead. For his middle-class family, members of one of this city's largest and most well-established clans, it was a disappointing choice. But more disappointment and hardship was to come.

Iyad's 14-year-old brother, Amjad, was shot by Israeli sol-diers in the courtyard near their house Jan. 3, during an Israeli raid in Nablus. At the funeral, Mr. Masri says, one of their cousins was also shot and killed while carrying Amjad's body to his grave.

"We knew [Iyad] was very sad. We told him, 'OK, it's terri-ble we lost your brother, but we'll find you a wife and build a house for you,'" says Masri, a clean-shaven man who does ac-counting for a local pharmacy. "I told him, 'We'll help you.' I tried to give him some hope."

> *'Out of the hopeless and the inhuman environment they live in, there is the promise that they will have a better life in heaven.'*

Iyad was already looking for it elsewhere. A week before his death, he went to a professional photo studio. Just before go-ing on suicide missions, would-be bombers often have themselves photographed with guns and Islamic imagery.

But in his last picture, Iyad looks more hip-hop than Hamas [a terrorist group], wearing a black ski hat and a sports jersey. His father doesn't believe that he meant it to be his last photo, but he cannot be sure. "How we know him is completely different from what he was inside, really," he says.

> *Just before going on suicide missions, would-be bombers often have themselves photographed with guns and Islamic imagery.*

It's the sort of comment that might be made by the parent of a teenager anywhere in the world. But here in particular, the question of where to place grief and anger is rarely discussed. At schools, the topic of suicide bombings is kept out of the curriculum entirely—although the Masris say it would be better if it were open for debate.

"It's a real problem here, that we can't talk about it," says Mr. Masri. "If you say you're for it [that is, suicide bombing], the Israelis will drag you away. But if you say you're against it, the whole community will isolate you."

"The right picture about our lives"

Yousef Aref, a teacher in Nablus, says he never broaches the subject of suicide bombings in school because he must check his politics at the door. Outside work, however, he is a prominent member of the political wing of Islamic Jihad, and speaks in defense of the assistance others in the organization gave to Iyad.

"When the people are under foreign occupation, there are no special rules to choose the strugglers in the resistance," says Mr. Aref between Arabic classes. On the wall of the school's administrative office, a crayon drawing by one of his students shows Israeli tanks and helicopters attacking Palestinian homes.

"Nobody is recruited by force—they come voluntarily. They don't recruit teenagers. But young teenagers are motivated and want to be recruited, so they put pressure on the older ones to recruit them," he says. The general guidelines are as follows: anyone under 20, an only son, or a young man who has lost his brother is supposed to be turned away. Or not.

"He [Iyad] was pushing for it," says Aref, a fair-skinned rotund man with a trim, white beard. "He wanted to be a suicide bomber. He threatened them [Islamic Jihad officials] and said, 'If you don't take me, I'll just go to others for help.'"

When the bombers are teenagers, he says, "it causes a catastrophe to the family. Palestinian organizations avoid recruiting them. But if they succeed, our society will see them as superheros."

Images of martyrs here are ubiquitous, appearing on bedroom walls where sports icons and movie stars might otherwise be. But Aref says he would encourage minors interested in martyrdom to be patient. "I tell them, 'It's early for you. You still have time. Wait.'"

On the steps of the Ar-Rawda School, which teaches students through their second year of college, most young men are quick to offer support to teenagers who become suicide bombers or otherwise participate in what is commonly known here as amiliyyat istishadiyye—martyrdom operations. "Two or three of my friends have been suicide bombers. It's a sad feeling because you lose a friend," says Mustafa Farah, a 20-year-old student. "But I also think it's good. It's an expression of emotions. It shows the world the right picture about our lives."

4

Despair and Hopelessness Do Not Motivate Suicide Bombers

Daniel Pipes

Daniel Pipes is director of the Middle East Forum, a board member of the U.S. Institute of Peace, and a prolific writer on current affairs.

Although conventional wisdom suggests otherwise, poverty, despair and hopelessness do not motivate people to become suicide bombers. In fact, many suicide bombers, such as the perpetrators of the September 11, 2001, terrorist attacks on America, are well-educated, middle-class people with jobs and families. Additionally, militant beliefs that lead to or encourage suicide terrorism are more prevalent in wealthier regions than in poorer ones. Suicide bombers are instead motivated by a revolutionary activism that finds fertile ground in prosperity and wealth. They seek power and glory that cannot be attained in the material world.

The events of September [11, 2001, when the United States was attacked by terrorists] have intensified a longstanding debate: What causes Muslims to turn to militant Islam? Some analysts have noted the poverty of Afghanistan [the base for the terrorists] and concluded that herein lay the problem. Jessica Stern of Harvard University wrote that the United States "can no longer afford to allow states to fail." If it does not devote a much higher priority to health, education and economic development abroad, she writes, "new Osamas [that is, terrorist imitating Osama bin Laden] will continue to arise." Susan Sachs of the *New York Times* observes: "Predictably, the disappointed youth of Egypt and Saudi Arabia turn to religion for comfort." More colorfully, others have advocated bombarding Afghanistan with foodstuffs not along with but instead of explosives.

Behind these analyses lies an assumption that socioeconomic distress drives Muslims to extremism. The evidence, however, does not support this expectation. Militant Islam (or Islamism) is not a response to poverty or impoverishment; not only are Bangladesh and Iraq not hotbeds of militant Islam, but militant Islam has often surged in countries experiencing rapid economic growth. The factors that cause militant Islam to decline or flourish appear to have more to do with issues of identity than with economics.

The conventional wisdom about despair and terrorism

The conventional wisdom—that economic stress causes militant Islam and that economic growth is needed to blunt it—has many well-placed adherents. Even some Islamists themselves accept this connection. In the words of a fiery sheikh from Cairo [Egypt], "Islam is the religion of bad times." A Hamas [terrorist group] leader in Gaza [a Palestinian territory], Mahmud az-Zahar, says, "It is enough to see the poverty-stricken outskirts of Algiers [Algeria] or the refugee camps in Gaza to understand the factors that nurture the strength of the [terrorist group] Islamic Resistance Movement.". . .

> *Conventional wisdom points to militant Islam attracting the poor, the alienated and the marginal—but research finds precisely the opposite to be true.*

Western politicians also find the argument compelling. For former President Bill Clinton, "These forces of reaction feed on disillusionment, poverty and despair," and he advocates a socioeconomic remedy: "spread prosperity and security to all."

Edward Djerejian, once a top [U.S.] State Department figure, reports that "political Islamic movements are to an important degree rooted in worsening socio-economic conditions in individual countries." Martin Indyk, another former high-ranking U.S. diplomat, warns that those wishing to reduce the appeal of militant Islam must first solve the economic, social and political problems that constitute its breeding grounds. . . .

> *These are not the children of poverty or despair.*

But the empirical record evinces little correlation between economics and militant Islam. Aggregate measures of wealth and economic trends fall flat as predictors of where militant Islam will be strong and where not. On the level of individuals, too, conventional wisdom points to militant Islam attracting the poor, the alienated and the marginal—but research finds precisely the opposite to be true. To the extent that economic factors explain who becomes Islamist, they point to the fairly well off; not the poor.

The conventional wisdom is wrong

Take Egypt as a test case. In a 1980 study, the Egyptian social scientist Saad Eddin Ibrahim interviewed Islamists in Egyptian jails and found that the typical member is "young (early twenties), of rural or small-town background, from the middle or lower middle class, with high achievement and motivation, upwardly mobile, with science or engineering education, and from a normally cohesive family." In other words, Ibrahim concluded, these young men were "significantly above the average in their generation"; they were "ideal or model young Egyptians." In a subsequent study, he found that out of 34 members of the violent group At-Takfir w'al-Hijra, fully 21 had fathers in the civil service, nearly all of them middle-ranking. More recently, the Canadian Security Intelligence Service found that the leadership of the militant Islamic group Al-Jihad "is largely university educated with middle-class backgrounds." These are not the children of poverty or despair.

Other researchers confirm these findings for Egypt. In a

study on the country's economic troubles, Galal A. Amin, an economist at the American University in Cairo, concludes by noting "how rare it is to find examples of religious fanaticism among either the higher or the very lowest social strata of the Egyptian population." When her assistant in Cairo turned Islamist, the American journalist Geraldine Brooks tells of her surprise: "I'd assumed that the turn to Islam was the desperate choice of poor people searching for heavenly solace. But Sahar [the assistant] was neither desperate nor poor. She belonged somewhere near the stratosphere of Egypt's meticulously tiered society." And note this account by the talented journalist Hamza Hendawi: In Egypt, a new breed of preachers in business suits and with cellular phones are attracting increasing numbers of the rich and powerful away from Western lifestyles and into religious conservatism. The modern imams [Islamic clergy] hold their seminars over banquets in some of Cairo's most luxurious homes and in Egypt's seaside resorts to appeal to the wealthy's sense of style and comfort.

"Money, education and privilege"

What is true of Egypt holds equally true elsewhere: Like [the uncompromising ideologies of] fascism and Marxism-Leninism in their heydays, militant Islam attracts highly competent, motivated and ambitious individuals. Far from being the laggards of society, they are its leaders. Brooks, a much-traveled journalist, found Islamists to be "the most gifted" of the youth she encountered. Those "hearing the Islamic call included the students with the most options, not just the desperate cases. . . . They were the elites of the next decade: the people who would shape their nations' future."

Even Islamists who make the ultimate sacrifice and give up their lives fit this pattern of financial ease and advanced education. A disproportionate number of terrorists and suicide bombers have higher education, often in engineering and the sciences. This generalization applies equally to the Palestinian suicide bombers attacking Israel and the followers of Osama bin Laden who hijacked the four planes on September 11. In the first case, one researcher found by looking at their profiles that: "Economic circumstances did not seem to be a decisive factor. While none of the 16 subjects could be described as well-off; some were certainly struggling less than others." In the second case, as the Princeton historian Sean Wilentz sardonically put it, the biographies of the September 11 killers would imply that the root cause of terrorism is "money, education and privilege." More generally, Fathi ash-Shiqaqi, founding leader of the arch-murderous [terrorist group] Islamic Jihad, once commented, "Some of the young people who have sacrificed themselves [in terrorist operations] came from well-off families and had successful university careers." This makes sense, for suicide bombers who hurl themselves against foreign enemies offer their lives not to protest financial deprivation but to change the world.

> *Militant Islam attracts highly competent, motivated and ambitious individuals.*

Those who back militant Islamic organizations also tend to be well off. They come more often from the richer city than the poorer countryside, a fact that, as Khalid M. Amayreh, a Palestinian journalist, points out, "refutes the widely-held assumption that Islamist popularity thrives on economic misery." And they come not just from the cities but from the upper ranks. At times, an astonishing one-quarter of the membership in Turkey's leading militant Islamic organization, now called the Saadet Party, have been engineers. Indeed, the typical cadre in a militant Islamic party is an engineer in his forties born in a city to parents who had moved from the countryside. Amayreh finds that in the Jordanian parliamentary elections of 1994, the [militant Islamic group] Muslim Brethren did as well in middle-class districts as in poor ones. He generalizes from this that "a substantial majority of Islamists and their supporters come from the middle and upper socio-economic strata."

Martin Kramer, editor of the *Middle East Quarterly*, goes further and sees militant Islam as the vehicle of counter-elites, people who, by virtue of education and/or income, are potential members of the elite, but who for some reason or another get excluded. Their education may lack some crucial prestige-conferring element; the sources of their wealth may be a bit tainted. Or they may just come from the wrong background. So while they are educated and wealthy, they have a grievance: their ambition is blocked, they cannot translate their socioeconomic assets into political clout. Islamism is particularly useful to these people, in part because by its careful manipulation, it is possible to recruit a following among the poor, who make valuable foot-soldiers. . . .

Not a product of poverty

The same pattern that holds for individual Islamists exists on the level of societies, as well. That social pattern can be expressed by four propositions.

First, wealth does not inoculate against militant Islam. Kuwaitis enjoy a Western-style income (and owe their state's very existence to the West) but Islamists generally win the largest bloc of seats in parliament (at present, twenty out of fifty). The West Bank [a Palestinian territory] is more prosperous than Gaza, yet militant Islamic groups usually enjoy more popularity in the former than the latter. Militant Islam flourishes in the member states of the European Union and in North America, where Muslims as a group enjoy a standard living higher than the national averages. And of those Muslims, as [author] Khalid Duran points out, Islamists have the generally higher incomes: "In the United States, the difference between Islamists and common Muslims is largely one between haves and have-nots. Muslims have the numbers; Islamists have the dollars."

> *A disproportionate number of terrorists and suicide bombers have higher education, often in engineering and the sciences.*

Second, a flourishing economy does not inoculate against radical Islam. Today's militant Islamic movements took off in the 1970s, precisely as oil-exporting states enjoyed extraordinary growth rates. [Libyan dictator] Muammar Qaddafi developed his eccentric version of proto-militant Islam then; fanatical groups in Saudi Arabia violently seized the Great Mosque of Mecca; and Ayatollah [Ruhollah] Khomeini took power in Iran (though, admittedly, growth had slacked off several years before he overthrew the Shah [the former king]). In the 1980s, several countries that excelled economically experienced a militant Islamic boom. Jordan, Tunisia and Morocco all did well economically in the 1990s—as did their militant Islamic movements. Turks under [Turkish prime minister] Turgut Ozal enjoyed nearly a decade of particularly impressive economic growth even as they joined militant Islamic parties in ever larger numbers.

Third, poverty does not generate militant Islam. There are many very poor Muslim states but few of them have become centers of militant Islam—not Bangladesh, not Yemen, and not Niger. As an American specialist rightly notes, "economic despair, the oft-cited source of political Islam's power, is familiar to the Middle East." If militant Islam is connected to poverty, why was it not a stronger force in years and centuries past, when the region was poorer than it is today?

Fourth, a declining economy does not generate militant Islam. The 1997 crash in Indonesia and Malaysia did not spur a large turn toward militant Islam. Iranian incomes have gone down by half or more since the [militant] Islamic Republic came to power in 1979; yet, far from increasing support for the regime's militant Islamic ideology, impoverishment has caused a massive alienation from Islam. Iraqis have experienced an even more precipitous drop in living standards: [economist] Abbas Alnasrawi estimates that per capita income has plummeted by nearly 90 percent since 1980, returning it to where it was in the 1940s. While the country has witnessed an increase in personal piety, militant Islam has not surged, nor is it the leading expression of anti-regime sentiments.

Noting these patterns, at least a few observers have drawn the correct conclusion. The outspoken Algerian secularist, Said Sadi, flatly rejects the thesis that poverty spurs militant Islam: "I do not adhere to this view that it is widespread unemployment and poverty which produce terrorism." Likewise, Amayreh finds that militant Islam "is not a product or by-product of poverty.". . .

A different argument

If poverty is not the driving force behind militant Islam, several policy implications follow. First, prosperity cannot be looked to as the solution to militant Islam and foreign aid cannot serve as the outside world's main tool to combat it. Second, Westernization also does not provide a solution. To the contrary, many outstanding militant Islamic leaders are not just familiar with Western ways but are expert in them. In particular, a disproportionate number of them have advanced degrees in technology and the sciences. It sometimes seems that Westernization is a route to hating the West. Third, economic growth does not inevitably lead to improved relations with Muslim states. In some cases (for example, Algeria), it might help; in others (Saudi Arabia), it might hurt.

> **"** Suicide bombers who hurl themselves against foreign enemies offer their lives not to protest financial deprivation but to change the world. **"**

Could it be quite contrarily, that militant Islam results from wealth rather than poverty? It is possible. There is, after all, the universal phenomenon that people become more engaged ideologically and active politically only when they have reached a fairly high standard of living. Revolutions take place, it has often been noted, only when a substantial middle class exists. Birthe Hansen, an associate professor at the University of Copenhagen, hints at this when she writes that "the spread of free market capitalism and liberal democracy . . . is probably an important factor behind the rise of political Islam."

Moreover, there is a specifically Islamic phenomenon of the faith having been associated with worldly success. Through history, from the Prophet Muhammad's time to the Ottoman Empire a millennium later, Muslims usually had more wealth and more power than other peoples, and were more literate and healthy. With time, Islamic faith came to be associated with worldly well-being. . . . This connection appears still to hold. For example, as noted in the formulation known as Issawi's law ("Where there are Muslims, there is oil; the converse is not true"), the 1970s oil boom mainly benefited Muslims; it is probably no coincidence that the current wave of militant Islam began then. Seeing themselves as "pioneers of a movement that is an alternative to Western civilization", Islamists need a strong economic base. As [Professor] Galal Amin writes, "There may be a strong relationship between the growth of incomes that have the nature of economic rent and the growth of religious fanaticism."

Conversely, poor Muslims have tended to be more impressed by alternative affiliations. Over the centuries, for example, apostasy from the religion has mostly occurred when things have gone badly. That was the case when Tatars fell under Russian rule or when Sunni [Muslim] Lebanese lost power to the Maronites [Lebanese Christians]. It was also the case in 1995 in Iraqi Kurdistan, a region under double embargo and suffering from civil war.

> *If militant Islam is connected to poverty, why was it not a stronger force in years and centuries past, when the region was poorer than it is today?*

Trying to live their lives in the midst of fire and gunpowder, Kurdish villagers have reached the point where they are prepared to give up anything to save themselves from hunger and death. From their perspective, changing their religion to get a visa to the West is becoming an increasingly more important option. There are, in short, ample reasons for thinking that militant Islam results more from success than from failure.

"The elevator to take power"

That being the likely case, it is probably more fruitful to look less to economics and more to other factors when seeking the sources of militant Islam. While material reasons deeply appeal to Western sensibilities, they offer little guidance in this case. In general, Westerners attribute too many of the Arab world's problems, observes David Wurmser of the American Enterprise Institute, "to specific material issues" such as land and wealth. This usually means a tendency "to belittle belief and strict adherence to principle as genuine and dismiss it as a cynical exploitation of the masses by politicians. As such, Western observers see material issues and leaders, not the spiritual state of the Arab world, as the heart of the problem." Or, in Osama bin Laden's ugly formulation, "Because America worships money, it believes that [other] people think that way too."

Indeed, if one turns away from the commentators on militant Islam and instead listens to the Islamists themselves, it quickly becomes apparent that they rarely talk about prosperity. As Iran's Ayatollah Khomeini memorably put it, "We did not create a revolution to lower the price of melon." If anything, they look at the consumer societies of the West with distaste. Wajdi Ghunayim, an Egyptian Islamist, sees it as "the reign of décolleté and moda [fashion]" whose common denominator is an appeal to the bestial instincts of human nature. Economic assets for Islamists represent not the good life but added strength to do battle against the West. Money serves to train cadres and buy weapons, not to buy a bigger house or a late-model car. Wealth is a means, not an end.

Means toward what? Toward power. Islamists care less about material strength than about where they stand in the world. They talk incessantly of this. In a typical statement, 'Ali Akbar Mohtashemi, the leading Iranian hardliner, predicts that "ultimately Islam will become the supreme power." Similarly, Mustafa Mashhur, an Egyptian Islamist, declares that the slogan "God is Great" will reverberate "until Islam spreads throughout the world." Abdessalam Yassine, a Moroccan Islamist, asserts "We demand power"—and the man standing in his way, the late King Hassan, concluded that for Islamists, Islam is "the elevator to take power." He was right. By reducing the economic dimension to its proper proportions, and appreciating the religious, cultural and political dimensions, we may actually begin to understand what causes militant Islam.

5

The Promise of an Afterlife Motivates Suicide Bombers

Raphael Israeli

*A former intelligence officer in the Israeli army, Raphael Is-
raeli is a professor of Islamic and Middle Eastern history at
Hebrew University in Jerusalem, Israel.*

Islamic suicide bombers become martyrs in order to
gain access to a heavenly paradise that is reportedly the
pinnacle of pleasure and enjoyment. In paradise the
martyr who has died for Islam supposedly drinks wine
that never causes a hangover and is married to seventy-
two beautiful virgins. Martyrs are exalted above all
other Muslims in heaven and are entitled to enjoy jewels, fine silk, sex, and alcohol for all of eternity. It is also
said that a martyr's actions can assure his or her relatives a space in paradise, which is another large draw for
Muslims eager to take care of their families. Terrorist
groups promulgate these beliefs about the afterlife
through songs, leaflets, speeches, and posters, thereby
encouraging Muslims to become martyrs.

B oth *shahid* [a martyr] and *fida'i* [a devoted assassin] are motivated by a profound and numbing religious fanaticism
which pushes them to commit acts of self-sacrifice, which we
usually refer to as 'suicide attacks', though they have nothing
to do with suicide. . . . In both cases . . . , the self-sacrificing
hero is assured of martyrdom and of very concrete rewards in
the hereafter, not only for himself, but also for his loved ones.

It is not uncommon, therefore, to witness hordes of well-wishers coming to the bereaved family of the martyr to express not condolences, but congratulations for the way their relative had paved for them the road to Paradise. In either case, the would-be killers have to be trained and prepared psychologically in such a fashion as to neutralize the normal human instincts for self-preservation, and to be able not only to defy death, but to be eager in the face of it. . . .

The lure of paradise

To induce a young Muslim to become an Islamikaze[1] his operators must first emasculate the natural fear of death that is innate in any human being. They may fascinate their naïve and adept novice by comparing the promised hereafter, where the would-be martyr is free of concern and pursues a rewarding and eternal material life depicted in lively colour and enveloped in lust and debauchery, with the hardships of his real life, which is full of pitfalls, frustrations and uncertainties, and fleeting in any case. He may be tempted to take a shortcut to Heaven to save himself the vagaries of his actual and temporary stay on earth. In April 1995, a poignant story was published in an Israeli newspaper concerning a young 15-year-old Palestinian boy from Gaza, whose quest to blow himself up among Israeli civilians had been foiled. He said during his police interrogation, 'We are born to die, and our lives are merely a transition to death and eternal life in Paradise. . . . Death is a good thing, not the bad, horrific and ugly thing that we were made to believe.'. . .

Indeed, in the world of the Islamikaze, the hereafter is lauded not as an escape, but as a desirable fulfilment. Paradise is unexpectedly depicted in exciting, plastic, worldly and pleasurable terms, not in some vague spiritual entity worthy of mystics or saints of other traditions. Sex and wine, the two foremost taboos in traditional Islamic society, are exalted in the Islamikaze popular literature as accessible and permissible in unlimited quantities, because in the hereafter, everything is in abundant and limitless supply and the restrictions of the worldly Shari'a [Islamic] law do not apply. More puzzling is the

1. The author is making a comparison to the Japanese suicide fighters known as kamikaze. Kamikaze pilots became famous during World War II when they deliberately crashed their planes into enemy ships, sacrificing their own lives to inflict damage upon their enemy.

fact that the public which extols the martyrs stands as an approving, envious and adoring audience in the face of the violation of their worldly Shari'a limitation, not as a traumatized or disgusted public, as in the case of cult-instigated massacres or plain suicide.

> *It is not uncommon . . . to witness hordes of well-wishers coming to the bereaved family of the martyr to express not condolences, but congratulations.*

The construct 'suicide bomber' has been used by Western media and the political community and, as such, it has had deleterious consequences: minimizing, trivializing and distorting a highly significant phenomenon. 'Suicide bomber' implies a disposition towards madness, yet it has not emanated from psychologically responsible sources. Turning to an Islamic frame of reference for a definition, and perhaps a diagnosis would, then, appear imperative if we are to comprehend the underlying motive for this sort of unparalleled mode of self-sacrifice. . . .

"Life with a Paradise girl"

Let us listen to a widely circulated tape extolling the Islamikaze:

    I Come on brother, join jihad [holy war]
       Carry your machine-gun from early morning
       And come brother, join jihad. Choose one of
          the two
       Either victory and a life of delight
       Or death and a life with a Paradise girl.[2]

    (Refrain)
    Oh brother! Your country calls upon you!
    Stand up and come to liberate her.
    Oh, Aqsa Mosque [in Jerusalem under Israeli
       control], we are all mourning

2. One of the reported rewards of paradise is that martyrs will be married to seventy-two beautiful virgins for all of eternity.

Your desecration by those cursed by Allah [the
  Jews].

II But when the Muslims take notice,
  You will bloom again like jasmine.
  Oh brother! We have already endured
    humiliation
  Look at Sabra and Mia Mia.[3]
  Manhood and zeal are lost
  Unless you pick up your machine-gun and join
    jihad.

The feeling of 'we have reached the ebb', 'we have nothing to lose' is exactly the impetus for exposing oneself to a certain death, either by self-immolation at the heart of the enemy, or in daring battle without chance of survival. For while 'here' there is only humiliation and suffering, 'there' [in Paradise] the promise is great, and still greater is the temptation to take a short-cut and get there as early as possible in one's life. Beyond this, one can detect in the song all three elements of the Islamikaze make-up: delegitimation of the enemy (the desecrators of al-Aqsa, who are cursed by Allah); the call for jihad, which binds all Muslim fighters, more so the fundamentalists who are not waiting for the established community or regime to launch it; and the final step of luring the predisposed to do so, to their death without fear and with great rewards awaiting the strong of heart. Here is another popular song of this sort:

The solution is inherent in your faith, your Islam,
  your weapons
Oh brother! Persist in your way, with
  determination and resolve
How sweet to the ear is the voice calling for
  jihad!
You better sing these lyrics of audacity
While handling the arrows in your quiver.
We shall crush the bastions of injustice
And turn them into ashes.
Then we shall brandish the banner of faith
With pride and fortitude.
We have come to you, the landscape of our
  country,

3. a reference to two Palestinian refugee camps that have been the scenes of death, poverty, and despair

Ready to defy death and to cleanse the impurities
Of the Zionist [that is, Israeli] enemies.

The link between self-sacrifice and daring in battle, and the
hereafter, had been established by a passage from the Qur'an
[the Muslim holy book], where the Prophet [Muhammad], who
was instigating his followers not to fear battle, lauded the next
world, which is 'incomparably better than this one'. This link
is further elaborated in the tradition related to the Angels
Munkir and *Nakir*, who reportedly interrogate every recently de-
ceased Muslim by making him traverse the purifying fire of
Heaven before he is admitted to Paradise. Reputedly, martyrs
will have saved themselves from the torments of that horrible
interrogation, both upon their arrival to Heaven, since they are
directly admitted to Paradise, and on the Day of Resurrection,
when all humans will resubmit to that frightening trial. A Hadith [a traditional story about the Prophet Muhammad], citing
the Prophet, specifies that the *shahid:*

> . . . will be pardoned [for his sins] by Allah, will
> take his place in Paradise, will be dressed with the
> Cloth of Faith, will marry beautiful-eyed young
> women, will be spared the torments of the tomb,
> will not submit to the Day of Judgement, and will
> have one of the world's best precious stones adorn
> his crown.

Martyrs are rewarded in Paradise

After admission into Paradise, the martyrs are blissfully rewarded by acquiring a higher position than all the other
dwellers, which enables them to partake of the eternal plea-
sures and delights that the place has to offer. The Holy Qur'an
abounds with exciting descriptions of the Garden of Eden,
where the climate is temperate—not a trifle for Arabs originat-
ing from the deserts of Arabia—and where they can indulge in
drink from silver cups, dressed in expensive silk, adorned with
silver jewels amidst gardens where wine flows like rivers. This
dream-like living is certainly mind-boggling inasmuch as it
provides a never waning source of happiness and bliss, as compared with worldly suffering, uncertainty and deprivation. It
was the Prophet himself who urged jihad fighters to distin-
guish themselves in battle, in view of what was awaiting them
in the quickly attainable hereafter. The position of the martyr

in Heaven is extolled, for his dwelling surpass[es] all the others, as it is located close to Allah's throne. Many Hadith elaborate on those magnificient descriptions, like the one painting Paradise in terms of a divine blinking light, branches of fragrant trees, flowing rivers, tall palaces, an abundance of fruit, luxurious clothes and exquisite women, which make for eternal, glorious, peaceful and plentiful living.

> **//** *'Death is a good thing, not the bad, horrific and ugly thing that we were made to believe.'* **//**

This mind-boggling mode of life, that is no doubt irresistible to the prospective martyr, also has a spiritual side. The *shahid* is considered a mediator for others to gain admission to Paradise, for after his death he can 'lobby' for others before the highest in Heaven. This striving on behalf of others, known in Islam as *shafa'a*, which for the most part has been reserved as a prerogative of the Prophet himself in Muslim tradition, was expanded to the martyr by scholars like Abu Talib, the Meccan, and the famous scholar and mystic, al-Ghazali. It is precisely the combination of sublime living and superior spiritual power which makes martyrdom a very sought-after and enviable status in normative Islam, let alone among the fundamentalist militants, whose sensitivity and proclivity to these promises makes them so popular and adulated, and role models to follow. If this needs to be stressed once again, this is what elevates the Islamikaze above and beyond regular fighters, and certainly distinguishes them from plain suicidal types or murderers in the eyes of non-Muslim societies. Under these cultural circumstances, martyrdom reads not as a hasty murderous act by a deranged individual who could not find his place in society, but as a supreme act by a worthy and chosen individual, who attains in one stroke what the living, even the most pious among them, cannot achieve by a lifetime of good deeds and saintly practices.

6

American Imperialism Motivates Suicide Bombers

Osama bin Laden

Osama bin Laden is the founder of the terrorist group al Qaeda. He is considered one of the most dangerous men in the world and is wanted by the U.S. government in connection with several terrorist attacks against the United States and its allies, including the September 11, 2001, attacks.

The United States has committed crimes against Islam, and thus all devout Muslims must wage war on America. The United States has insulted Islam by establishing military bases in the Holy Land of Saudi Arabia. The United States has also sought to destroy the nation of Iraq and control other Arab nations in order to gain access to Middle Eastern oil. Moreover, its unrelenting support of Israel humiliates Muslims everywhere. With these actions, the United States has declared war on God and is in partnership with the devil. Muslims are thus justified in declaring holy war against the United States. It is the duty of every Muslim in the world to kill Americans in order to restore honor and dignity to the Middle East and to Islam.

Praise be to God, who revealed the Book [the Koran], controls the clouds, defeats factionalism, and says in His Book "But when the forbidden months are past, then fight and slay the pagans wherever ye find them, seize them, beleaguer them, and lie in wait for them in every stratagem (of war)"; and peace

Osama bin Laden, "Text of Fatwah Urging Jihad Against Americans," *al-Quds al-'Arabi*, February 23, 1998.

be upon our Prophet, Muhammad Bin-'Abdallah, who said "I have been sent with the sword between my hands to ensure that no one but God is worshipped, God who put my livelihood under the shadow of my spear and who inflicts humiliation and scorn on those who disobey my orders." The Arabian Peninsula has never—since God made it flat, created its desert, and encircled it with seas—been stormed by any forces like the crusader armies [that is, American troops] now spreading in it like locusts, consuming its riches and destroying its plantations. All this is happening at a time when nations are attacking Muslims like people fighting over a plate of food. In the light of the grave situation and the lack of support, we and you are obliged to discuss current events, and we should all agree on how to settle the matter.

American aggression must be stopped

No one argues today about three facts that are known to everyone; we will list them, in order to remind everyone:

First, for over seven years the United States has been occupying the lands of Islam in the holiest of places, the Arabian Peninsula, plundering its riches, dictating to its rulers, humiliating its people, terrorizing its neighbors, and turning its bases in the Peninsula into a spearhead through which to fight the neighboring Muslim peoples.

If some people have formerly debated the fact of the occupation, all the people of the Peninsula have now acknowledged it.

The best proof of this is the Americans' continuing aggression against the Iraqi people using the Peninsula as a staging post, even though all its rulers are against their territories being used to that end, still they are helpless. Second, despite the great devastation inflicted on the Iraqi people by the crusader-Zionist alliance[1] and despite the huge number of those killed, in excess of 1 million . . . despite all this, the Americans are once again trying to repeat the horrific massacres, as though they are not content with the protracted blockade imposed after the ferocious war or the fragmentation and devastation.

So now they come to annihilate what is left of this people and to humiliate their Muslim neighbors.

Third, if the Americans' aims behind these wars are religious and economic, the aim is also to serve the Jews' petty

1. the alliance between the United States and Israel

state and divert attention from its occupation of Jerusalem and murder of Muslims there.

The best proof of this is their eagerness to destroy Iraq, the strongest neighboring Arab state, and their endeavor to fragment all the states of the region such as Iraq, Saudi Arabia, Egypt, and Sudan into paper statelets and through their disunion and weakness to guarantee Israel's survival and the continuation of the brutal crusade occupation of the Peninsula.

> *The Arabian Peninsula has never—since God made it flat, created its desert, and encircled it with seas—been stormed by any forces like the crusader armies [that is, American troops] now spreading in it.*

All these crimes and sins committed by the Americans are a clear declaration of war on God, his messenger, and Muslims. And ulema [the Islamic community of scholars] have throughout Islamic history unanimously agreed that the jihad [holy war] is an individual duty if the enemy destroys the Muslim countries. This was revealed by Imam Bin-Qadamah in "Al-Mughni," Imam al-Kisa'i in "Al-Bada'i," al-Qurtubi in his interpretation, and the shaykh of al-Islam in his books, where he said "As for the militant struggle, it is aimed at defending sanctity and religion, and it is a duty as agreed. Nothing is more sacred than belief except repulsing an enemy who is attacking religion and life."

Kill the Americans and their allies

On that basis, and in compliance with God's order, we issue the following fatwa [edict] to all Muslims:
The ruling to kill the Americans and their allies—civilians and military—is an individual duty for every Muslim who can do it in any country in which it is possible to do it, in order to liberate the al-Aqsa Mosque [in Jerusalem] and the holy mosque [in Saudi Arabia] from their grip, and in order for their armies to move out of all the lands of Islam, defeated and unable to threaten any Muslim. This is in accordance with the words of Almighty God, "and fight the pagans all together as they fight

you all together," and "fight them until there is no more tumult or oppression, and there prevail justice and faith in God."

This is in addition to the words of Almighty God "And why should ye not fight in the cause of God and of those who, being weak, are ill-treated and oppressed—women and children, whose cry is 'Our Lord, rescue us from this town, whose people are oppressors; and raise for us from thee one who will help!'"

We—with God's help—call on every Muslim who believes in God and wishes to be rewarded to comply with God's order to kill the Americans and plunder their money wherever and whenever they find it. We also call on Muslim ulema, leaders, youths, and soldiers to launch the raid on Satan's U.S. troops and the devil's supporters allying with them, and to displace those who are behind them so that they may learn a lesson.

Almighty God said "O ye who believe, give your response to God and His Apostle [the prophet Muhammad] when He calleth you to that which will give you life. And know that God cometh between a man and his heart, and that it is He to whom ye shall all be gathered."

Almighty God also says "O ye who believe, what is the matter with you, that when ye are asked to go forth in the cause of God, ye cling so heavily to the earth! Do ye prefer the life of this world to the hereafter? But little is the comfort of this life, as compared with the hereafter. Unless ye go forth, He will punish you with a grievous penalty, and put others in your place; but Him ye would not harm in the least. For God hath power over all things."

Almighty God also says "So lose no heart, nor fall into despair. For ye must gain mastery if ye are true in faith."

7

Nationalism Motivates Suicide Terrorists

Robert A. Pape

In addition to being a leading expert in the field of suicide terrorism, Robert A. Pape is a political science professor at the University of Chicago.

Contrary to popular perception, suicide bombers are not overwhelmingly motivated by religion, despair, or the promise of an afterlife, but by nationalism. In fact, the most active suicide terrorist group—the Tamil Tigers of Sri Lanka—is not religious. Most suicide terrorist groups are primarily motivated by a desire to form their own country and oust what they perceive to be foreign invaders from land they claim as their own. Moreover, suicide terrorists are not irrational fanatics; they have carefully concluded that suicide terrorism is the best way to coerce their enemy to concede territory or grant nationhood. The use of suicide terrorism is thus a strategic method aimed toward securing nationalist goals.

Terrorist organizations are increasingly relying on suicide attacks to achieve major political objectives. For example, spectacular suicide terrorist attacks have recently been employed by Palestinian groups in attempts to force Israel to abandon the West Bank and Gaza, by the Liberation Tigers of Tamil Eelam to compel the Sri Lankan government to accept an independent Tamil homeland, and by [the terrorist group] Al Qaeda to pressure the United States to withdraw from the Saudi Arabian Peninsula. Moreover, such attacks are increasing both in tempo and location. Before the early 1980s, suicide terrorism

Robert A. Pape, "The Strategic Logic of Suicide Terrorism," *American Political Science Review*, vol. 97, August 2003, pp. 343–44, 345, 348–49. Reproduced by permission of Cambridge University Press.

was rare but not, unknown. However, since the attack on the U.S. embassy in Beirut [Lebanon] in April 1983, there have been at least 188 separate suicide terrorist attacks worldwide, in Lebanon, Israel, Sri Lanka, India, Pakistan, Afghanistan, Yemen, Turkey, Russia and the United States. The rate has increased from 31 in the 1980s, to 104 in the 1990s, to 53 in 2000–2001 alone. The rise of suicide terrorism is especially remarkable, given that the total number of terrorist incidents worldwide fell during the period, from a peak of 666 in 1987 to a low of 274 in 1998, with 348 in 2001.

Religious fanaticism does not explain most suicide terrorism

What accounts for the rise in suicide terrorism, especially, the sharp escalation from the 1990s onward? Although terrorism has long been part of international politics, we do not have good explanations for the growing phenomenon of suicide terrorism. Traditional studies of terrorism tend to treat suicide attack as one of many tactics that terrorists use and so do not shed much light on the recent rise of this type of attack. The small number of studies addressed explicitly to suicide terrorism tend to focus on the irrationality of the act of suicide from the perspective of the individual attacker. As a result, they focus on individual motives—either religious indoctrination (especially Islamic Fundamentalism) or psychological predispositions that might drive individual suicide bombers.

> **//** *Suicide terrorists can be college educated or uneducated, married or single, men or women, socially isolated or integrated, from age 13 to age 47.* **//**

The first-wave explanations of suicide terrorism were developed during the 1980s and were consistent with the data from that period. However, as suicide attacks mounted from the 1990s onward, it has become increasingly evident that these initial explanations are insufficient to account for which individuals become suicide terrorists and, more importantly, why terrorist organizations are increasingly relying on this form of attack. First, although religious motives may matter, modern suicide terrorism is not limited to Islamic Fundamentalism. Islamic groups receive the most attention in Western media, but the world's leader in suicide terrorism is actually the Liberation Tigers of Tamil Eelam (LTTE), a group who recruits from the predominantly Hindu Tamil population in northern and eastern Sri Lanka and whose ideology has Marxist/Leninist elements [that is, nonreligious roots]. The LTTE alone accounts for 75 of the 186 suicide terrorist attacks from 1980 to 2001. Even among Islamic suicide attacks, groups with secular orientations account for about a third of these attacks.

> *The most important goal that a community can have is the independence of its homeland (population, property, and way of life) from foreign influence or control.*

Second, although study of the personal characteristics of suicide attackers may someday help identify individuals terrorist organizations are likely to recruit for this purpose, the vast spread of suicide terrorism over the last two decades suggests that there may not be a single profile. Until recently, the leading experts in psychological profiles of suicide terrorists characterized them as uneducated, unemployed, socially isolated, single men in their late teens and early 20s. Now we know that suicide terrorists can be college educated or uneducated, married or single, men or women, socially isolated or integrated, from age 13 to age 47. In other words, although only a tiny number of people become suicide terrorists, they come from a broad cross section of lifestyles, and it may be impossible to pick them out in advance. . . .

Suicide bombers are not irrational

Most suicide terrorism is undertaken as strategic effort directed toward achieving particular political goals; it is not simply the product of irrational individuals or an expression of fanatical hatreds. The main purpose of suicide terrorism is to use the threat of punishment to coerce a target government to change policy, especially to cause democratic states to withdraw forces from territory terrorists view as their homeland. The record of suicide terrorism from 1980 to 2001 exhibits tendencies in the timing, goals, and targets of attack that are consistent with this strategic logic but not with irrational or fanatical behavior. . . .

If suicide terrorism were mainly irrational or even disorganized, we would expect a much different pattern in which either political goals were not articulated (e.g., references in news reports to "rogue" attacks) or the stated goals varied considerably even within the same conflict. We would also expect the timing to be either random or, perhaps, event-driven, in response to particularly provocative or infuriating actions by the other side, but little if at all related to the progress of negotiations over issues in dispute that the terrorists want to influence.

Suicide bombers have nationalist goals

Suicide terrorism is a high-cost strategy, one that would only make strategic sense for a group when high interests are at stake and, even then, as a last resort. The reason is that suicide terrorism maximizes coercive leverage at the expense of support among the terrorists' own community and so can be sustained over time only when there already exists a high degree of commitment among the potential pool of recruits. The most important goal that a community can have is the independence of its homeland (population, property, and way of life) from foreign influence or control. As a result, a strategy of suicide terrorism is most likely to be used to achieve nationalist goals, such as gaining control of what the terrorists see as their national homeland territory and expelling foreign military forces from that territory.

> *Since 1980, there has not been a suicide terrorist campaign directed mainly against . . . opponents who did not have military forces in the terrorists' homeland.*

In fact, every suicide campaign from 1980 to 2001 has had as a major objective—or as its central objective—coercing a foreign government that has military forces in what they see as their homeland to take those forces out. . . . Since 1980, there has not been a suicide terrorist campaign directed mainly against domestic opponents or against foreign opponents who did not have military forces in the terrorists' homeland. Although attacks against civilians are often the most salient to Western observers, actually every suicide terrorist campaign in the past two decades has included attacks directly against the foreign military forces in the country, and most have been waged by guerrilla organizations that also use more conventional methods of attack against those forces.

> *The terrorists are simply the members of their societies who are the most optimistic about the usefulness of violence for achieving goals that many, and often most, support.*

Even Al Qaeda fits this pattern. Although Saudi Arabia is not under American military occupation per se and the terrorists have political objectives against the Saudi regime and others, one major objective of Al Qaeda is the expulsion of U.S. troops from the Saudi Peninsula and there have been attacks by terrorists loyal to Osama Bin Laden against American troops in Saudi Arabia. To be sure, there is a major debate among Islamists over the morality of suicide attacks, but within Saudi Arabia there is little debate over Al Qaeda's objection to American forces in the region and over 95% of Saudi society reportedly agrees with Bin Laden on this matter.

Still, even if suicide terrorism follows a strategic logic, could some suicide terrorist campaigns be irrational in the sense that they are being waged for unrealistic goals? The answer is that some suicide terrorist groups have not been realistic in expecting the full concessions demanded of the target, but this is normal for disputes involving overlapping nationalist claims and even for coercive attempts in general. Rather, the ambitions of terrorist leaders are realistic in two other senses. First, suicide terrorists' political aims, if not their methods, are often more mainstream than observers realize; they generally reflect quite common, straightforward nationalist self-determination claims of their community. Second, these groups often have significant support for their policy goals versus the target state, goals that are typically much the same as those of other nationalists within their community. Differences between the terrorists and more "moderate" leaders usually concern the usefulness of a certain level of violence and—sometimes—the legitimacy of attacking additional targets besides foreign troops in the country, such as attacks in other countries or against third parties and civilians. Thus, it is not that the terrorists pursue radical goals and then seek others' support. Rather, the terrorists are simply the members of their societies who are the most optimistic about the usefulness of violence for achieving goals that many, and often most, support.

8

Anti-Semitism Motivates Suicide Bombers

Fiamma Nirenstein

Fiamma Nirenstein is an Italian journalist based in Jerusalem, Israel. She is the author of the book Israel: Peace in War.

Anti-Semitic propaganda abounds in the Arab world. Middle Eastern schools, television and radio stations, newspapers, and government agencies all go to great lengths to demonize Jews in order to create a common enemy for the Arab world to unite against. Lies include accusing Israelis of spreading drugs, disease, and chemical weapons among the Palestinians. Jews are even accused of using the blood of Gentiles to prepare their food. Unsurprisingly, Arabs come to believe that Jews must be destroyed at all costs. Suicide bombers are thus easily recruited to attack Israel, believing that Israeli Jews are devils that need to be killed in the name of God.

During his historic visit to Syria last May [2001], Pope John Paul II was unexpectedly upstaged by the country's young new president, Bashar al-Assad. Greeting the pontiff at the airport in Damascus, Assad used the occasion not to declare his own hopes for mutual understanding among the world's great faiths but—rather less in keeping with the spirit of the moment—to mount a vicious attack on the Jews. They have "tried," he inveighed in the presence of the Pope, "to kill the principles of all religions with the same mentality with which they betrayed Jesus Christ," and in "the same way they tried to betray and kill the prophet Muhammad."

Fiamma Nirenstein, "How Suicide Bombers Are Made," *Commentary*, vol. 112, September 2001, p. 53. Copyright © 2001 by the American Jewish Committee. Reproduced by permission of the publisher and the author.

So spectacular a venting of hate could hardly pass unnoted, and thus, for the duration of a news cycle, the usual fare of Middle East reporting—rock-throwers and settlers, bombings and retaliatory strikes, ceasefires and "confidence-building" measures—gave way to tongue-clucking over the charged words of the Syrian president. As the *New York Times* lamented, Assad had not only "marred" the Pope's visit but had reinforced his own "growing reputation for irresponsible leadership." So the coverage generally went, admonishing a new leader whose inexperience and immaturity had seemingly led him to embrace, as the *Times* put it, "bigotry."

> *Wherever one looks . . . the very people with whom the state of Israel is expected to live in peace have devoted themselves with ever-greater ingenuity to slandering and demonizing the Jewish state.*

Largely ignored amid all this was a far bigger story—a story not about a petty tyrant but about the poison that rose so readily to his lips. As few journalists either knew or thought it worthwhile to relate, such sentiments as Assad expressed are hardly uncommon in today's Arab world. Wherever one looks, from Cairo [Egypt] and Gaza [in the Palestinian territories] to Damascus [Syria] and Baghdad [Iraq], from political and religious figures to writers and educators, from lawyers to pop stars, and in every organ of the media, the very people with whom the state of Israel is expected to live in peace have devoted themselves with ever-greater ingenuity to slandering and demonizing the Jewish state, the Jewish people, and Judaism itself—and calling openly for their annihilation. Only by turning a determinedly blind eye to this river of hatred is it possible to be persuaded that, after all, "everybody" in the Middle East really wants the same thing.

Vicious lies about Jews abound

The anti-Semitic propaganda that circulates in such abundance in the Arab world draws its energy in large part from the technique of the "big lie"—that is, the insistent assertion of outrageous falsehoods about Israel or the Jews, the more outrageous the better. The examples are truly numberless. In Egypt and Jordan, news sources have repeatedly warned that Israel has distributed drug-laced chewing gum and candy, intended (it is said) to kill children and make women sexually corrupt. When foot-and-mouth disease broke out . . . among cattle in the Palestinian Authority (PA), the Israelis were quickly accused of intentionally spreading the illness (despite the immediate mobilization of Israeli veterinary groups to treat the animals).

Especially garish have been the fabrications directed at Israel's response to the . . . intifada [recent Palestinian uprising]. Earlier this year, at the world economic forum in Davos, Switzerland, a thunderstruck audience heard [Palestinian leader] Yasir Arafat himself declare that Israel was using depleted uranium and nerve gas against Palestinian civilians. Official PA television obligingly furnished "evidence" for this charge, broadcasting scenes of hapless victims racked by vomiting and convulsions. Another recent film clip from Palestinian television offered a "re-enactment" of an assault by the Israeli army on a Palestinian house, culminating in the staged rape and murder of a little girl in front of her horrified parents. As for Israeli victims of Arab terrorists, the PA's Voice of Palestine radio assured its listeners in April that Israel was lying about the assassination of a ten-month-old girl by a Palestinian sniper in Hebron; in fact, the commentator explained, the baby was retarded and had been smothered by her own mother.

> *In Egypt and Jordan, news sources have repeatedly warned that Israel has distributed drug-laced chewing gum and candy, intended (it is said) to kill children and make women sexually corrupt.*

The Arab press has also helped itself to the rich trove of classical European anti-Semitism. Outstanding in this regard has been *Al-Ahram*, Egypt's leading government-sponsored daily. One recent series related in great detail how Jews use the blood of Gentiles to make matzah for Passover. Not to be outdone, columnist Mustafa Mahmud informed his readers that, to understand the true intentions of the Jews, one must consult The Protocols of the Elders of Zion, in which the leaders of the international Jewish conspiracy acknowledge openly their "limitless ambitions, inexhaustible greed, merciless vengeance, and hatred beyond imagination. . . . Cunning," they allegedly declare, "is our approach, mystery is our way."

> *The Arab press has also helped itself to the rich trove of classical European anti-Semitism.*

In a class of its own is the effort of Arab and Islamic spokesmen to distort or dismiss the record of Nazi genocide. Indeed, nowhere else in the world is Holocaust denial more warmly or widely espoused. A conference of "scholars" held in Amman [Jordan] in mid-May [2001] concluded that the scope of the Nazi war against the Jews had been greatly exaggerated, a claim enthusiastically parroted by the *Jordan Times*. On Palestinian television, Issam Sissalem of the Islamic University of Gaza recently asserted that, far from being extermination camps, Chelmo, Dachau, and Auschwitz were in fact mere "places of disinfection."

On April 13 [2001]—observed in Israel as Holocaust Remembrance Day—the official Palestinian newspaper *Al-Hayat al-Fadida* featured a column by Hiri Manzour titled "The Fable of the Holocaust." Among his claims: that "the figure of 6 million Jews cremated in the Nazi Auschwitz camps is a lie," promulgated by Jews in order to carry out their "operation of international marketing." A few weeks later, at a well-attended pan-Islamic conference in Teheran [Iran], Iran's supreme leader, the Ayatollah Khomenei, used his opening remarks to make a similar point. "There is proof," he declared, "that the Zionists [proponents of Israel] had close ties with the German Nazis, and exaggerated all the data regarding the killing of the Jews . . . as an expedient to attract the solidarity of public opinion and smooth the way for the occupation of Palestine and the justification of Zionist crimes."

Occasionally, to be sure, the same organs of anti-Semitic opinion that deny the Holocaust do find it necessary to affirm that it took place—but only so that they can laud its perpetrators. A columnist in Egypt's government-sponsored *Al-Akhbar* thus expressed his "thanks to Hitler, of blessed memory, who on behalf of the Palestinians took revenge in advance on the most vile criminals on the face of the earth. Still, we do have a complaint against [Hitler], for his revenge on them was not enough."

Another variation on this theme is the now incessant comparison of Israel itself to Hitlerite Germany. In the eyes of *Al-Ahram*, "the atrocities committed by the Israeli army show . . . how those who complain about Nazi practices use the same methods against the Palestinians." For its sister Egyptian paper, *Al-Akhbar*, the ostensibly dovish Israeli foreign minister Shimon Peres is in actuality "a bird of prey, a master in the killing of the innocents," and a man responsible for deeds that "make Israel worse than the Nazis." In May, a columnist for Egypt's *Al-Arabi* wrote, "Zionism is not only another face of Nazism, but rather a double Nazism." Unsurprisingly, President Assad of Syria also favors such language, recently asserting that "Israel is racist, [Prime Minister Ariel] Sharon is racist, the Israelis are racist. They are more racist than the Nazis."

Anti-Semitism produces suicide bombers

The effect of this relentless vilification is not difficult to discern. In the Arab world, where countervailing sources of information about Jews and the Jewish state are rare to non-existent, Israel has been transformed into little more than a diabolical abstraction, not a country at all but a malignant force embodying every possible negative attribute—aggressor, usurper, sinner, occupier, corrupter, infidel, murderer, barbarian. As for Israelis themselves, they are seen not as citizens, workers, students, or parents but as the uniformed foot soldiers of that same dark force. The uncomplicated sentiment produced by these caricatures is neatly captured by the latest hit song in Cairo, Damascus, and East Jerusalem. Its title: "I Hate Israel."

> *From such hatred it is but a short step to incitement and acts of violence.*

From such hatred it is but a short step to incitement and acts of violence. Arab schools teach not just that Israel is evil, but that extirpating this evil is the noblest of callings. As a text for Syrian tenth graders puts it, "The logic of justice obligates the application of the single verdict [on the Jews] from which there is no escape: namely, that their criminal intentions be turned against them and that they be exterminated." In Gaza and the West Bank, textbooks at every grade level praise the young man who elects to become a shahid, a martyr for the cause of Palestine and Islam.

The lessons hardly stop at the classroom door. Palestinian television openly urges children to sacrifice themselves. In one much-aired film clip, an image of twelve-year-old Mohammed al-Dura—the boy killed last September [2000] in an exchange of fire between Israeli soldiers and Palestinian gunmen—appears in front of a landscape of paradise, replete with fountains and flowers, beckoning his peers to follow.

> **❝One need look no further to understand how children grow up wanting to be suicide bombers.❞**

In early June, just two weeks after the fatal collapse of a Jerusalem wedding hall, PA television broadcast a sermon by Sheikh Ibrahim Madhi praying that "this oppressive Knesset [the Israeli parliament] will [similarly] collapse over the heads of the Jews" and calling down blessings upon "whoever has put a belt of explosives on his body or on his sons and plunged into the midst of the Jews." Slogan-chanting mass demonstrations, with Israeli and American flags aflame and masked gunmen firing shots into the air, reinforce the message. One need look no further to understand how children grow up wanting to be suicide bombers—a pursuit that won a fresh wave of media acclaim after a bombing at a Tel Aviv discotheque took 21 Israeli lives and that according to a recent poll has the approval of over three-quarters of Palestinians. "This missile," wrote an ecstatic Palestinian columnist, meaning the bomber himself, "carried a soul striving for martyrdom, a heart that embraces Palestine, and a body that treads over all the Zionist invaders."

Virulent anti-Semitism is no less essential in maintaining the region's most militant and totalitarian-minded regimes. Such standing as Syria's Bashar Assad now enjoys in the wider Arab world derives in large part from his unceasing denunciations of Israel and the Jews. . . .

As for "moderates" like King Abdullah of Jordan and President [Hosni] Mubarak of Egypt, offering a wide latitude to anti-

Semitic vituperation enables them to demonstrate their own populist bona fides, to show their sympathy with the Arab "street." Do they themselves endorse such views? Of course not, they hasten to declare, disingenuously suggesting that nothing can be done about it since under their regimes even government-owned newspapers and television stations possess the right to speak their mind.

World leaders must not excuse rampant anti-Semitism

That moderate Arab leaders have remained mum in the face of rising anti-Semitism may be all too understandable, considering their overall records as statesmen. The West's moral and political leaders should be another matter, but they are not. In the days after Assad's anti-Semitic diatribe in Damascus, one waited in vain for the Pope—the same Pope who has recognized the state of Israel and visited the Holocaust memorial in Jerusalem—to utter a word of protest. The incident was, in many respects, a replay of then-First Lady Hillary Clinton's refusal to confront Suha Arafat when, at an event in Ramallah two years ago, the wife of the PA's president accused Israel of deliberately poisoning Palestinian air and water. And if any of the assembled leaders at the world economic conference in Davos thought to protest Yasir Arafat's lies publicly, their intervention has not been recorded.

One source of the general silence may be a subtle form of racism, or what [U.S. president] George W. Bush in another context called "the soft bigotry of low expectations." The Arabs, it is implicitly suggested, are a backward people, not to be held to the civilized standards of the West. In this reading, rabid anti-Semitism is just another feature of Arab culture—the same ancient culture that is often also portrayed, with reason, as one of the world's most civilized and sophisticated.

Many Westerners who fastidiously ignore the Arabs' outrageous lies and insults about Jews also believe that the Arabs do, after all, have a legitimate grievance against Israel, however excessively they may at times express it. Once the substantive demands of the Palestinians or the Syrians are met, this line of thought goes, their hatred of Israel and the Jews will likewise subside, it being just a form of politics by other means. Throughout the Oslo [peace summits of the 1990s], the government of Israel itself seemed to share this attitude, systematically ignoring or explaining away the Arabs' unremitting verbal incitement.

But if we have learned nothing else from the latest intifada, it is that the Arab world's grievance against Israel has little to do with the minutiae of dividing up territory and political authority. It has to do instead with the entire Zionist project, with the very existence of a Jewish state in the Middle East. What Westerners (including some Israelis) dismiss as so much unfortunate rhetoric is an exact articulation of that grievance, whose goal is not to achieve but to prevent accommodation. For how can one accommodate a people who are nothing but murderers of children, instruments of world conspiracy, sworn enemies of religious and historical truth, and perfecters of Nazi brutality—a people who according to Islamic authorities must be driven out and killed, their body parts "spread all over the trees and electricity poles"? No, anti-Semitism in the Middle East is not just politics by other means; it is an end in itself.

9

Islamic Schools Groom Suicide Bombers

Ben Barber

Before becoming a correspondent for the Washington Times *in 1994, Ben Barber was a freelance journalist for the* London Observer, *the* Christian Science Monitor, *the* Baltimore Sun, *and other publications.*

Islamic schools called madrasahs train students to participate in jihad, or holy war, and to become martyrs who will die in the name of Islam. Madrasahs are plentiful in Muslim countries such as Pakistan, where a regular education is too expensive for most people to afford. Madrasahs also offer students meals, free clothing, and a place to sleep, which is usually more than their families can provide for them. In these schools, young Muslims are encouraged to give up their lives in defense of Islam. They are also taught that people of other religions must be converted to Islam. After years of such training, they are sent to fight holy wars in places around the world. Madrasahs are responsible for training most of the world's terrorists, including the suicide hijackers who perpetrated the September 11, 2001, terrorist attacks on America.

It was hard to imagine that the smiling children playing a quick game of cricket on a rooftop courtyard in the heart of Pakistan's ancient cultural capital of Lahore were learning to be killers.

The head of their madrasah (religious school), a portly man with a white turban and white Pakistani clothing, had invited me to see for myself how his students were treated and what they had learned. So I'd climbed some steps in the Khuddamud-din madrasah, one of perhaps 7,000 such religious schools in Pakistan, and found the boys at play, taking a break from classes.

In a few moments chatting with them, I quickly learned that their major topic of study was jihad, or holy war. The nearly 2,000 students expect to fight infidels in Chechnya, Afghanistan, Palestine, or Indian Kashmir once they complete their studies at the madrasah, located inside the walls of the old city of Lahore.

This school and others like it have prospered in recent years, in part because of the failure of the state-run educational system. In Pakistan, the illiteracy rate among adults is estimated at 70 percent.

> **❝** *The system of madrasahs has become a hatchery for tens of thousands of Islamic militants who have spread conflict around the world.* **❞**

About 1.75 million students are enrolled in the schools, though it is not clear how many of the academies are devoted to preparing their students for jihad. Some may focus only on religious studies. It is certain, however, that each time the repressive Islamic Taliban regime in Afghanistan[1] needs to mount a spring offensive against its rebel opponents, tens of thousands of students from Pakistani madrasahs pour over the border in trucks to join the jihad, according to reports. . . .

Thus, the system of madrasahs has become a hatchery for tens of thousands of Islamic militants who have spread conflict around the world. Incidents in the Philippines, Indonesia, Russia, Central Asia, and at New York's World Trade Center [on September 11, 2001] have all been linked to graduates of the madrasahs. Indeed, Pakistan is terrorism's fertile garden.

Khuddamuddin is run by Mohammed Ajmal Qadri, leader of one of the three branches of the fundamentalist Jamiat Ulema Islam party, who told me that nearly 13,000 trained jihad fighters have passed through his school. At least 2,000 of

---

1. The Taliban regime was deposed in the fall of 2001. However, students of madrasahs continue to travel to Afghanistan to fight the government that was put in place by the United States.

them were in or on their way to Indian-held Kashmir [which is also claimed by Pakistan].

Converting the world to Islam

Qadri, polite and well spoken in the British-accented English of South Asia, offered an American guest tea and then calmly disclosed that the modern concepts of tolerance and cultural understanding have not made inroads into his thinking.

"Eventually, all people must become Muslim, including the Christians and Jews of the United States," he said in an interview. "The world has to go the way we want. It's our divine right to lead humanity." He apologized for a lack of time to spend with a visitor, saying he was preparing for yet another of his frequent visits to the United States. There, he preaches in the hundreds of new mosques built in the last decade by Muslim immigrants and raises money for his school—where he teaches his children to kill those who stand in the path of Islamic dominance in the world.

Up on the stone rooftop courtyard of his 110-year-old school, the students were taking advantage of a free period to hit a cricket ball, run, and wrestle like children anywhere in the world. But one slightly built boy explained how he and his classmates were being directed toward a life of violent struggle.

"Most kids here go for jihad, and I will too, God willing," said 14-year-old Obeidulla Anwer, speaking in Urdu through a translator. "Jihad is to fight for Islam and the pride of Islam."

> *'Eventually, all people must become Muslim, including the Christians and Jews of the United States.'*

Like most of his classmates, he will leave the school at about age 18 and go to a military training camp in Pakistani-controlled Kashmir, Afghanistan, or some other secret location. After that training, he said, "We go to fight in Kashmir, Chechnya, Palestine, Afghanistan."

Asked whether he was prepared to hurt or kill, the delicate, dark boy said: "I will hurt those who are enemies of Islam. And I know that I could be hurt or killed."

The chances that Obeidulla will die violently are high. A 23-year-old fighter with another Islamic militant group, Hizbul Mujahideen, said that five of the eight young men in his squad had died during his 18 months of fighting against Indian troops in Kashmir, where an estimated 30,000 people have died in civil strife since 1989.

Obeidulla was asked how he would recognize the enemies of Islam. "If I greet them with 'Salam Aleikum' and they won't say it back," he answered.

> *The children all sleep on the floor of the school's mosque in sleeping bags, which they roll up each morning. They rise at 3:00 A.M. for study and prayers.*

The boy was asked: "Since most Americans do not know Arabic and cannot know how to respond to the traditional Muslim greeting, are they enemies of Islam?" The boy looked confused. "I don't know," he said, looking expectantly at his hovering teachers, who also appeared confused by the question. Asked directly whether all non-Muslims were anti-Muslim, he did not need to check with his teachers. "No," he said firmly.

The school is preparing Obeidulla and his classmates for the hard life of soldiers with an experience that provides little comfort or privacy. The children all sleep on the floor of the school's mosque in sleeping bags, which they roll up each morning. They rise at 3:00 A.M. for study and prayers with a break for play around 4:30 A.M. At 7:30, they have breakfast and then study until 11:00, when they sleep for two hours.

They pray, study, have lunch, pray, study, and pray again until dinner at 9:30 P.M., after which they go to the mosque to sleep. They have no room or even a bed of their own.

Why madrasahs thrive

Parents choose this hard life for their children for a variety of reasons, with religious conviction and the poverty of village life both playing major roles.

Religion dominates life in Pakistan, where the national airline begins its flights with a reading from the Qur'an [the Muslim holy book] or a prayer. Politicians, even those educated in London or Boston and living apparently Westernized lives, vie in calling for stricter Islamic laws.

Poverty is the other goad. A half-hour drive from Lahore and just a stone's throw from the Indian border crossing at Wagha, farmer Mohammed Shaffi explained why his 13-year-old son attends the local madrasah and not a public school.

In the madrasah—many are funded by donations from Saudi Arabia and other Muslim nations or groups in wealthy countries—he memorizes the Qur'an in Arabic, which he cannot understand. But he is not being taught to read and write the national language, Urdu.

"How can a poor man educate his son?" asked Shaffi, leaning for a moment over the mud wall he was building around his tiny rice paddy in the village of Dayal, about 30 miles southeast of Lahore. "Even if the school is free, the books are not. And the paper."

> *With the drumbeat of resurgent Islam in the air and hopes of a good job slim for an illiterate youth from the countryside, jihad is not an unlikely choice.*

Shaffi, whose younger son was playing nearby stark naked, did not even mention the cost of school clothes. As he spoke, a herd of cows ambled by his naked child, who scratched at the muddy earth with a sharp stick. Another son, 13-year-old Maratab Ali Shaffi, wore a filthy, torn pair of shorts as he helped his mother and father pack mud upon a brick wall to increase its height.

The farmer said it was too early to make a decision about letting the boy go and join a jihad. But with the drumbeat of resurgent Islam in the air and hopes of a good job slim for an illiterate youth from the countryside, jihad is not an unlikely choice.

The family has two acres of land, on which six-inch-tall rice plants waved above the flooded paddies. They have electricity but can afford only two lightbulbs. They have no radio or television. No one in the family can read or write. The local madrasah, by contrast, will provide Maratab a free daily meal and sometimes a free shirt.

"A divine gift for Americans"

In Lahore, Qadri said he is proud that his school is able to direct youths like Maratab into holy war in places like Chechnya and Kashmir. But it is America that seems to be his ultimate target, one he hopes to defeat through converting its people to Islam.

"There are now over 3,000 mosques and madrasahs in America, and they are a divine gift for Americans. American civilization . . . is empty and hollow from inside. Islam is the only cultural system that could bear the load of life for the times to come."

He was similarly dismissive of Hinduism, the religion of about 900 million people in neighboring India, describing it as nothing more than a system "of fashions and traditions."

Qadri said he would defy attempts by Pakistan's military government to regulate the madrasahs, beginning with a requirement that they report on the numbers and names of students and teachers, types of facilities, educational programs, and financial details.

The government, stung by charges from U.S. officials that it allows Islamic terrorism to breed under the guise of religious education, has also called for the schools to begin offering practical subjects such as math and science as well as memorization of the Qur'an. In addition, the government is asking the schools to report to local police the names of any foreign students and to list any religious rulings (fatwas) they issue.

"We believe our rules are perfect, and we will not allow any ruler, military, or so-called elected representatives to change them," Qadri said.

10

Television Influences Suicide Bombers

Patrick Sookhdeo

Patrick Sookhdeo is director of the Institute for the Study of Islam and Christianity, which monitors Christian groups in the Muslim world. He is also the author of several books, including A Christian's Pocket Guide to Islam.

Suicide bombers are motivated by extremists who televise anti-Western and anti-Israel propaganda all over the world. These satellite broadcasts reach Muslims living in many countries, motivating them to travel abroad to become suicide bombers. Carefully manipulated images of violence, injustice, and hate are transmitted nonstop on certain radical networks. Such persistent broadcasts create a community of angry Muslims who begin to believe that the Western world is against them.

Driving through the streets of Baghdad [Iraq] last week [May 2003], I was struck by the number of satellite dishes for sale everywhere. After years in which the appliances were banned by [former Iraqi dictator] Saddam [Hussein], freedom is sprouting all over the skyline. There is still an almost total absence of local media, so that Iraqis know nothing of what is going on in their own country except by rumour. But those who can afford a dish are eagerly beginning to learn about the world. They can get the BBC, CNN and even the Fox Channel; though these are not, alas, the only ones they are watching. Unless we are careful, we are about to lose a crucial propaganda war.

Broadcasts from the Middle East

I myself flicked through the channels on the rather antiquated television set in my room at the Baghdad Sheraton and found broadcasts from Abu Dhabi [United Arab Emirates] and from Iran. I watched footage of ayatollahs [Shiite Islamic religious leaders] in southern Iraq and images of the Palestinians suffering at the hands of the Israelis. I sat there captivated by the repeated, stylised pictures: a boy throwing stones at an Israeli tank; the Israelis moving in and shooting; the bulldozing of Palestinian homes. Then there was the Arabic-language news from the Qatar-based Al-Jazeera [news network] and from its new Dubai-based rival, Al-Arabiya. If [Iranian-backed terrorist group] Hezbollah's channel is not yet bringing Iraqis its regular shots of black-clad marching soldiers of Allah, it cannot be long.

What we too often fail to grasp is that these and similar channels are also on offer in the UK, and are widely watched. Whatever we may think of the merits of Western television, we must accept that, in many Muslim minds, it is tainted, in Britain as much as in Iraq. They may see the odd black or Asian newscaster; but every time an expert opinion is canvassed, the face of that expert is white. Like it or not, there is a prejudice that our channels are just propaganda for whites, or even under Zionist [that is, Israeli] control. I speak as an Asian, the son of Muslim parents from India and Pakistan. I may be an Anglican priest, but a large proportion of my immediate family support [Saudi-born terrorist Osama] bin Laden, and I hope I speak with some authority.

> *Suicide bombers act in concert with others who share their values and ideologies, shaping and reinforcing each other's attitudes.*

We cannot shirk the influence of television in trying to answer the question that arose recently: how two decent, middle-class young men of the Muslim faith, regarded as moderates by those who knew them, could leave the shores of Britain, travel to Israel with the intention of becoming martyrs, and in the process kill and injure many people whom they had never met and who had done them no wrong.

To most non-Muslim Britons it seems incomprehensible as well as abhorrent. For mainstream Muslim spokesmen, it is a denial of authentic Islam, which they claim condemns violence and the taking of innocent life. For Muslim radicals, however, there is clear justification in that Jews are held to be enemies of Islam. For the Muslim majority in Britain, who knows?

> *This programming deliberately creates and nurtures an image of 'the enemy', which is communicated to viewers every day.*

No one knows either how many other potential suicide bombers there are among the British Muslim community. Tens? Hundreds? Thousands? It is certain, however, that whatever motivated Asif Mohammed Hanif and Omar Khan Sharif, they are not the only Muslims in Britain to feel that way.

Creating an enemy

Suicide bombers act in concert with others who share their values and ideologies, shaping and reinforcing each other's attitudes. Passions are aroused, anger fuelled, and energies directed towards a given end. For this to happen an enemy must be created—a target for the hatred—who will later be crushed and destroyed.

For Hanif and Sharif, the cause was Palestine and the enemy was 'the Jew'. Although these two appear to have been radicalised and groomed for martyrdom while visiting Damascus [Syria], the seeds of hatred could have been sown at home in Britain. Suleiman Chachia, chairman of the trustees of the mosque in Hounslow which was attended by Hanif, has pinpointed the role of television news in stirring up Muslim passions, even to the point of creating suicide bombers. '[Muslim] people are very much concerned about Palestine. We see the killings on television, and to us a Palestinian death and an Israeli death is the same. But why are the United Nations resolutions not applied to Israel? This is a burning issue that has to be settled. Otherwise there will be other young men like this. What I know about Asif Hanif is that his nature was not aggressive.'

In thousands of Asian British homes the choice of viewing

is normally determined by the older generation, who in Asian culture make all decisions of any consequence in the home. These older family members, usually first- or second-generation immigrants, feel strong ties to their homeland. Their identity and their empathies lie there, not in Britain. They may find the English language difficult—some older women speak very little English despite having lived here for decades. Naturally they prefer to watch Pakistani and other Asian channels. Though the younger generation may like to watch British television when they are allowed to, most of what they hear and see in the home—even if unwillingly—emanates from Asia. It is these programmes which are discussed at meal times, or with friends, and thus attitudes are formed.

> *In any area where Muslims are seen to suffer, in any place where Muslims are said to be oppressed, a new enemy image can be discovered.*

The national television station of Pakistan plays an important role in creating opinion among Asian Muslims in Britain. Launched in 1964 with the motive of enabling the government to communicate with the largely illiterate masses, it is still very much controlled by the Pakistani government. News and other programmes from Pakistan television are broadcast on the satellite channels Prime TV and ARY, which are watched by many British Asians. This programming deliberately creates and nurtures an image of 'the enemy', which is communicated to viewers every day, as described by I.A. Rehman, director of the Pakistan Human Rights Commission, in his 2001 paper 'Enemy Images on Pakistan Television'.

The principal enemy, as presented by Pakistan television, is India, with virtually every news bulletin focusing on [Kashmir, which is disputed territory]. The enemy image is communicated by means of crude stereotypes that are almost caricatures—the cowardly, devious Indians versus the courageous, upright Pakistanis. The secondary enemy are the colonial masters who ruled south Asia for two humiliating centuries, i.e., Britain. The same message is conveyed in films. These creations are not just singing, dancing and romance; many also contain much violence and often an anticolonial, anti-British stance.

These issues are expanded by Pakistan television to embrace the whole Muslim cause. Britain is depicted as the enemy that extinguished the Muslim Mogul empire whose successor is considered to be Pakistan. Historical features examine the collapse of the Mogul empire, the attempted defence of the Turkish caliphate, the Pakistan movement, the origins of the Kashmir issue, etc. Even the Crusades and the expulsion of the Muslims from Spain in the 15th century are included in the general theme of the Christians versus the Muslim community worldwide.

Crushed like an ant

This has further developed into what is now seen as a war against Islam and the development of an Islamic identity and consciousness. The enemy is portrayed in many different contemporary forms. In the Palestinian context, tyrannous enemy Jews are depicted oppressing Muslim brothers and sisters. In the wars in Afghanistan and Iraq and the war on terrorism, the enemy has become the USA, Britain and the West in general. In every war of secession where Muslims seek independence, in any area where Muslims are seen to suffer, in any place where Muslims are said to be oppressed, a new enemy image can be discovered.

There is little or no attempt to analyse causes or to be guided by reason rather than by emotion. The enemy has no personality or identity, but is completely dehumanised so as to be crushed like an ant under foot without compunction.

> *One of the features of Islamic television is the video of the suicide bomber's last prayers. Like the Western wedding video, this has some formulaic elements.*

During the [2003] Iraq war, Al-Jazeera used the same method. Coalition troops [mostly American and British] were portrayed as inhuman enemy invaders, the camera lingering with apparent delight on coalition dead and gloating over prisoners of war. Long, drawn-out shots of wounded Iraqi children underlined the message that 'the enemy has done this' and is to be treated mercilessly in return.

One of the features of Islamic television is the video of the suicide bomber's last prayers. Like the Western wedding video, this has some formulaic elements: the bomber will be seen at prayer; he will be dressed in white; there will be a message for his family; and then, once he has done his work, there will be the shots of brutal Israeli reprisals. Never do such channels call him and his kind suicide bombers; they are shahid, or martyrs. Nor is there any condemnation offered in the commentary.

> *The attitudes of Muslim young people born and bred in Britain are being shaped by influences from outside which affect their identity and their ultimate loyalties.*

It is but a small step from this kind of material to the training of terrorists and suicide bombers, a large part of which is concerned with increasing their hatred and rage towards the enemy. [Osama bin Laden's terrorist group] Al-Qa'eda training videos portray the injuries and sufferings of Muslims, especially children. Suicide bombers are never sent to reconnoitre their targets, for fear that they would be touched by compassion for those they are to kill.

A variety of propaganda programming

While south Asians comprise the largest grouping within the British Muslim community, there is plenty of television for other Muslims also. Arabs can choose between news channels with varying stances. Al-Jazeera goes for comment and controversy, while Al-Arabiya aims to present the news straight and factually. So-called 'music videos' are often screened, glamorising the Palestinian conflict with slo-mo[tion] footage, or a montage of images shown to stirring music. Hezbollah's programmes are similar, cleverly reinforcing in the viewer's mind and heart the message of Palestinian suffering which must be avenged.

For Iranians in Britain, there is the Islamic Republic of Iran Broadcasting (Irib); most of its programmes are in [the Iranian language of] Farsi but there is also one in Arabic, thus increasing its potential audience many-fold (to include for example the Shias of southern Iraq). The international version of Irib is slightly different from what is broadcast within Iran itself. Much of Irib's airtime is devoted to Islamic teaching, upholding Islamic values and showing the corruption and immorality of the infidel West. Without actually urging Iranians to take up arms, the channel leaves no doubt as to who the villains are. Sermons at Friday noon prayers can be somewhat more explicit with, say, senior Islamic clerics exhorting Iranians to do what the Palestinians have done. An Iranian businessman in the UK told me that young Iranians in the West are fairly immune to this kind of propaganda as they basically prefer the freedoms of the West to the restrictions of the Islamic Republic of Iran. But what of the next generation, those who will have grown up here without even knowing life in Iran? They are likely to be seeking to return to their roots, based on their historical and religious identity. Will television teach them to despise the West and seek a solution in Islam?

> *If there is one step we should take urgently, it is to set up a Muslim station to broadcast sense and moderation.*

Today's emphasis on multiculturalism, which regards all histories, cultures and religions as equal within the British context, poses an increasingly serious problem. Modern multiculturalism defines ethnic identity very much in terms of its history and religion. Thus it encourages the rediscovery of historical background, culture and religion. The attitudes of Muslim young people born and bred in Britain are being shaped by influences from outside which affect their identity and their ultimate loyalties. Television is increasingly being used to reinforce this and to sell a message of repression and liberation; if they are taught to consider the land in which they live as the enemy, what future do we have?

Those who exploit the effect of the visual image on susceptible young people are well aware of how powerful it is, in that 'seeing is believing'. While we may have laws governing what is shown on terrestrial [that is, domestic] television, there is no way to limit what is beamed in from elsewhere. Even here in leafy Wiltshire I could view all these programmes if I chose to subscribe. Prime TV costs only 10 [pounds Sterling] a month. Free and unrestricted airwaves can communicate not only pornography and hedonistic materialism, but also religious radicalism. Ultimately the control will lie with those who hold the television remote-control in their hand—usually the older family members. How far will the average Muslim grandparent now take responsibility for that control?

If there is one step we should take urgently, it is to set up a Muslim station to broadcast sense and moderation to Iraq. One day, with any luck, that station will also be picked up in Britain.

11

Children Are Indoctrinated to Become Suicide Bombers

Kenneth R. Timmerman

Kenneth R. Timmerman is a writer for Insight *magazine.*

Palestinian children become suicide bombers after being carefully indoctrinated into a culture of martyrdom. The Palestinian Authority, the operating authority in the occupied territories of the West Bank and Gaza Strip, hires professional filmmakers to produce videos and music montages that make heroes and role models out of suicide bombers. Children are continuously exposed to these videos in order to groom them for martyrdom. This practice is not only abhorrent for its promotion of suicide terrorism, but it is the ultimate form of child abuse; defenseless, impressionable youth are brainwashed by calculating adults with political motives. Suicide bombing will continue as long as these impressionable children continue to be taught to glorify suicide bombing.

The five-minute video clip could have been produced by Jennifer Lopez to the music of Pink Floyd. It is professional, dreamy and haunting. It begins with a handsome young schoolboy writing a farewell letter to his parents. In this pop saga the boy goes off on a "mission" in which he dies, and his farewell letter is handed to his father, who tears his hair at the news. Scenes of the boy's last day scroll across the screen as an enchanting male voice puts the words of his letter to a haunting melody. "Do not be sad, my dear, and do not cry over my parting. Oh, my dear father; how sweet is Shahada [martyrdom]. How sweet is Shahada when I embrace you, oh my land."

> *In the video . . . his death is gentle, innocent, heroic—not at all the brutal dismemberment that awaits suicide bombers.*

In the video the boy embraces the ground with his arms stretched out as upon a cross. His death is gentle, innocent, heroic—not at all the brutal dismemberment that awaits suicide bombers. "Mother, my most dear, be joyous over my blood," he sings. "And do not cry for me."

That same line, "Mother, do not cry for me," has appeared in at least three farewell letters from 14- to 17-year-old Palestinians who have carried out suicide bombings since the film clip first aired on Palestinian television in May 2001, says Itamar Marcus, an Israeli researcher who unearthed the music videos. [Palestinian leader] Yasser Arafat's official TV station broadcast the dreamy clip virtually every day for more than a year in a clear effort to incite children to murder/suicide. It aired between cartoons, after school and in the early evening between regularly scheduled programs. . . .

The Palestinian Authority glorifies martyrdom

"For the six years we'd been following PA [Palestinian Authority] TV, we'd seen on average 15 minutes of violent, anti-Israeli and anti-Semitic video clips, interspersed between regular programming throughout the day," Marcus tells *Insight* [magazine] in Jerusalem. "Suddenly, in the summer of 2000, it went up to two hours per day, just as [former Israeli prime minister Ehud] Barak was getting ready to give away 98 percent of the territory the PA wanted at Camp David."

In the beginning, the violent trailers mostly were composed of old news footage edited to glamorize suicide bombings and to call people to the streets. But soon, professional filmmakers were called in to take advantage of their special skills.

Twelve-year-old Mohammad al-Dura is the most famous Palestinian "martyr." Images captured live by a Palestinian film crew and broadcast by French state-owned television on Oct. 2, 2000, show the boy shot to death in his father's arms, presumably by Israeli soldiers. Now he has become the posthumous star of a five-minute film clip produced and edited by Arafat's official state-owned TV. The opening screen is a handwritten message "signed" by the young Mohammad: "I am waving to you not to say goodbye, but to say, follow me." A child actor depicts the death of the young Mohammad, said to have been "massacred" by Israeli soldiers, then portrays him in paradise, riding on a Ferris wheel, flying a kite and playing on the beach. A haunting lyric accompanies these pictures, with lines including the following: "How sweet is the fragrance of the Shahids [martyrs]. How sweet is the scent of the earth, its thirst quenched by the gush of blood flowing from the youthful body." Then the vocalist does repeats with a choir:

> *A child actor depicts the death of the young Mohammad . . . then portrays him in paradise, riding on a Ferris wheel, flying a kite and playing on the beach.*

Vocalist: "Oh father; till we meet. Oh father; till we meet. I shall go with no fear, no tears. How sweet is the fragrance of the Shahids."

Choir: "How sweet is the fragrance of the Shahids.". . .

"These are the most evil films we ever saw," Marcus tells *Insight* as he plays a selection of these video clips, with English subtitles provided by his [organization] Palestinian Media Watch.

One of the many myths spread by leftwing academics and apologists for terrorism is that suicide bombers come from poor families where "hopelessness" drives them to despair and suicide. But, ever since Israel and the Clinton administration brought Arafat to Gaza in July 1994, he has been fostering hatred of Jews and promoting the cult of martyrdom through the schools, the mosques and the state-owned media. In eight years, the virus has infected all sectors of Palestinian society.

"The new role model for young Palestinian women is Wafa Idriss, the first female suicide bomber," Marcus says. Idriss blew herself up in Jerusalem on Jan. 27, 2002, killing an 81-year-old Israeli man and wounding 150 others, four seriously. "We're beginning to see her name pop up everywhere," Marcus says. "There's the Wafa Idriss course in human rights and democracy at Al-Quds University in Jerusalem. There are Wafa Idriss schools run by the United Nations. It's incredible."

"Shahada is very, very beautiful"

On June 9, 2002, two well-dressed 11-year-old girls named Wala and Yussra were interviewed on a talk show broadcast by PA TV about their personal yearning to achieve death through Shahada, which they said is the desire of "every Palestinian child." These were not children of the [refugee] camps, but from the middle classes. They explained that their goal was not to become doctors or teachers, but to achieve a proper death through martyrdom for Allah.

Host: "You described Shahada as something beautiful. Do you think it is beautiful?"

Wala: "Shahada is very, very beautiful. Everyone yearns for Shahada. What could be better than going to paradise?"

Host: "What is better, peace and full rights for the Palestinian people, or Shahada?"

Wala: "Shahada. I will achieve my rights after becoming a Shahida."

Yussra: "Of course Shahada is a good thing. We don't want this world; we want the afterlife. We benefit not from this life, but from the afterlife. The children of Palestine have accepted the concept that this is Shahada, and that death by Shahada is very good. Every Palestinian child aged, say 12, says: 'Oh Lord, I would like to become a Shahid.'"

'These are the most evil films we ever saw.'

Yet another film clip aimed at children intersperses scenes of "martyred" children about to be buried with normal street scenes of children playing. It ends with a black screen stamped with the official crest of the PA and a slogan in Arabic with its English translation: "Ask for death, the life will be given to you."

There is no precedent for this type of indoctrination. "Not

even Hitler did this," Marcus says. "The Hitler Youth were taught to kill, not to be killed. This is the ultimate in child abuse. Here you have a whole generation of kids who think the most they can accomplish in life is to die for Allah. This is a tragedy with implications that no one in the West has begun to contemplate."

The indoctrination of children is hard to stop

Some Palestinian parents have tried to raise their voices against the barbarity of the PA indoctrination, but to little effect. Bassam Zakhout is the father of a 14-year-old boy who set off in April [2002] with two schoolmates to attack an Israeli military outpost near the Netzarim settlement in Gaza. Prompted by the calls to martyrdom the three teen-agers armed themselves with knives and packed their schoolbags with explosives, apparently given to them by [the terrorist organization] Hamas, and ran across open ground toward the army post, where they were gunned down. Bassam Zakhout blamed PA TV for inciting the attack. "I am against all this, especially at his age," he said. "We should not destroy this generation. They are the leaders of the future."

After plastering Gaza with posters of the three "martyrs," Hamas was too embarrassed to claim responsibility once it heard the father's remark. "The blood of our cubs should be preserved for a coming day when they become strong men," said a Hamas statement issued soon afterward. "Their role in jihad [holy war] is for later." Even Arafat's deputy education minister, Naim Abu-Hummos, decried their deaths. "What's happening is crazy," he said, vowing to instruct Palestinian teachers to stop glorifying martyrs.

But those thoughts, if sincere, were short-lived. Addressing a chanting auditorium full of children in August [2002], Arafat put an end to any doubts: "Oh, children of Palestine! The colleagues, friends, brothers and sisters of Faris Ouda [a 14-year-old who died in the conflict]. The colleagues of this hero represent this immense and fundamental power that is within, and it shall be victorious, with Allah's will! One of you, a boy or a girl, shall raise the [Palestinian] flag over the walls of Jerusalem, its mosques and its churches. . . . Onward together to Jerusalem!"

12

Chechen Women Are Increasingly Recruited to Become Suicide Bombers

Kim Murphy

Kim Murphy is a staff writer for the Los Angeles Times.

Chechen women are becoming attracted to suicide terrorism. Over thirty female suicide bombers have launched attacks against Russians since 1999 in the hopes of helping fellow Chechens establish an independent Muslim state in the Russian-occupied region of Chechnya. These women are usually recruited into terrorist groups by strange and shadowy figures, such as the mysterious woman known as "Black Fatima." Sometimes they have lost husbands or children in the war and are seeking revenge on Russian soldiers and civilians. Others have been traumatized by the Russian military, which routinely kidnaps and tortures Chechen civilians and destroys their homes. Still other women are drugged and brainwashed into becoming suicide bombers for the Chechen cause.

Medna Bayrakova remembers the day a middle-aged woman showed up at her door and asked to speak to her 26-year-old daughter. They shut themselves in the bedroom for half an hour, and then her daughter left, saying she was walking the visitor to the bus stop.

An hour later, Zareta still hadn't returned and several men

in camouflage knocked at the door of the family's ravaged apartment in this ruined Chechen capital.

"We have taken away your daughter. She has agreed to marry one of our men," one said.

> **" A nationwide alert has been issued for a middle-aged woman with a hooked nose and dark hair popularly known as 'Black Fatima.'** **"**

Bayrakova protested. "She's a sick girl. She has tuberculosis. She was coughing up blood only this morning."

"We will cure her," they replied quietly.

The next time Bayrakova and her husband saw their daughter's face, it was 24 days later—separatist Chechen rebels had seized Moscow's Dubrovka Theater, along with 800 hostages. Zareta's unmistakable dark eyes were visible above a black veil on the television screen. Her fingers were clasped below a belt of powerful explosives. . . .

The "black widows" of Chechnya

In strapping the explosives belt to her waist that fall day in 2002, Zareta Bayrakova joined the cult of the "black widows," the female suicide bombers who have left much of Russia on wary watch for the mysterious, dark-eyed woman in a long fur coat who is believed to recruit them.

A nationwide alert has been issued for a middle-aged woman with a hooked nose and dark hair popularly known as "Black Fatima," who has been identified as a recruiter for the women known as shahidas, or martyrs. The woman reportedly has been seen lurking on the edges of terrorist bombings during a decade of tensions between Russia and the breakaway republic of Chechnya. Russian troops pulled out of the republic after a disastrous 1994-96 war, and the mostly Muslim region exercises self-rule. . . .

More than three dozen Chechen women—roughly half of the suicide bombers—have launched or attempted attacks against Russian targets since the second Chechen war began in 1999. Russian authorities say many appear to be dazed and under the influence of drugs; some would-be bombers have reported that they were forced by relatives in the Chechen resistance into attempting such attacks.

Most recently, on Dec. 9 [2003], a young woman blew herself up in front of Moscow's historic National Hotel, killing six people. An older woman in a dark coat and fur hat reportedly was seen slipping away from the scene. On Dec. 5 [2003], suicide bombers blew up a commuter train in the southern region of Stavropol, killing at least 44 others and injuring more than 150. Authorities said three women and one man were involved in the attack.

Nearly 150 people died in black-widow attacks [in the summer of 2003]—so named in the Russian media because many of the female perpetrators have lost husbands, brothers and fathers in the war in Chechnya.

What motivates the black widows?

Abu Walid, a Saudi national who is one of many Arabs who have joined the Chechen militants, is believed to be the commander of the rebels' eastern front in Chechnya. He recently explained the use of female suicide bombers in an interview with the Al Jazeera television network.

"These women, particularly the wives of the moujahedeen [Islamic fighters] who are martyred, are being threatened in their homes. Their honor and everything are being threatened," he said. "They do not accept being humiliated and living under occupation. They say that they want to serve the cause of almighty God and avenge the death of their husbands and persecuted people.". . .

Chechen rebels say the Russians are ignoring the deep domestic rage that motivates suicide attacks.

> *Chechen terrorists have attacked rock concerts, subway stations and commuter trains full of students.*

"The Chechens do not have the right to stain with their blood the streets of Russian cities, which are rear bases of the aggressors' army?" the Chechen separatist website, Kavkaz Center, asked sarcastically. "A Russian tank driver, with intestines of

Chechen children on its caterpillar track, and the pilot of a low-flying warplane shelling a bus with women and infants, are just unscrupulous uses of force, while a Chechen widow blowing herself up together with the pilots who have murdered her children is terrorism and cannot be justified.

"According to their logic, the Chechen nation must die magnanimously and in silence."

"We can't live like this anymore"

On a quiet side street in the former Cossack village of Asinovskaya in western Chechnya, there is a pile of rubble that used to be Sulumbek Ganiyev's house. It is the house in which he raised six sons and four daughters.

Only four children are alive, two of whom are in captivity. [His son] Islam was killed in a rocket attack in 1999. Daughter Petimat disappeared in July 2000 and is believed to have died in a bombing raid in Grozny. Rustam, a former rebel fighter, is in prison in North Ossetia. Hussein was fighting with the rebels when he was killed in 2000. Raisa, who resisted being recruited by her brother as a black widow, is being held by the Russian secret services at an undisclosed location. The youngest son, Tarkhan, died in a car accident. . . .

> *'How can you uncover a terrorist if she looks like everybody else?'*

Daughters Fatima and Khadzhad died in the Dubrovka Theater siege, with unused explosives belts strapped around their waists. . . .

[Their mother] Lyuba Ganiyev tried to explain what drove Fatima, a law student who often helped her father bale hay, and Khadzhad, who had hoped to become a gynecologist, to join the terrorists in Moscow—and [their sister] Raisa, who eventually turned herself in to Russian authorities, to nearly follow them.

"After [the Russians] beat them for three days, they had had enough. They came back and said, 'We are now in shame. They held us for three days. We can't live like this anymore.' It's not that they were crying. We never saw them crying. They were just sitting down, depressed."

On Sept. 29, 2002—the same day Zareta Bayrakova disappeared—Fatima and Khadzhad left home, saying they were going to Dagestan to see their nephew. They never returned. Their parents next saw them, as Medna Bayrakova had seen her daughter, a month later in television footage of the Dubrovka siege.

"They didn't tell us," Ganiyev said. "If we had known, we wouldn't have let them. I would have broken their legs to stop them.". . .

Violence on both sides

Russia has been widely criticized for atrocities and human rights violations—Chechen men and women have been regularly kidnapped from their homes, tortured and even killed—but the Russian public sees a military body count that often reaches half a dozen a day, as soldiers are ambushed in the hills or blown up by roadside explosive devices.

Chechen terrorists have attacked rock concerts, subway stations and commuter trains full of students. At the National Hotel, horrified witnesses described seeing severed heads and limbs strewn on the sidewalk. Others waited in fear for the next strike.

"We were immediately told on the radio that we should stand here and watch very, very carefully over the people who come here, because there was information that there are three other suicide bombers. So I am standing here breaking my eyes over everybody who comes in here," Yevgeny Petrov, a 23-year-old security guard, said as he anxiously watched passersby at a shopping center across the street on the morning of the hotel bombing.

"They told us they are women, and they will be constantly talking on the phone, as if somebody is hypnotizing them. Or we should look people in the eye, because their eyes will be weird, as if they are drugged," he said. "It's very scary. How can you uncover a terrorist if she looks like everybody else?"

"A virtual slave"

After the hotel bombing, a composite drawing was distributed, purported to be a likeness of Black Fatima. By then, everyone in Moscow knew who she was, mostly thanks to Zarema Muzhikhoyeva, a would-be black widow who [in July 2003] set

out to blow herself up at a restaurant on Moscow's Tverskaya
Street. . . .

Muzhikhoyeva, whose husband was killed fighting the war
while she was pregnant with their daughter, told her inter-
rogators that she had been "a virtual slave" to rebels who con-
vinced her that it was her religious duty to go to Moscow and
detonate a bomb at a cafe on busy Tverskaya Street. Investiga-
tors told the Moscow paper *Kommersant* that a woman
Muzhikhoyeva knew as Lyuba—Black Fatima—took her to a
house near Moscow and visited her frequently during the next
week. She told police that Lyuba often gave her orange juice
that made her dizzy and gave her a headache.

> *'You've been a sinner all your life. Allah
> punished you by taking your husband. Now it's
> time to restore yourself by doing your duty.'*

On the last day, she said, Lyuba gave her more juice,
handed her a [backpack] containing a bomb and showed her
how to set it off.

In a jailhouse interview published . . . in the newspaper
Izvestia, Muzhikhoyeva said two Chechen men prepared her
for the task and dropped her off near the cafe. After being con-
fronted by three men, she said, she went back on the street.

She said she had already decided not to pull the switch but
feared that her trainers would set it off by remote control.

"Neither I nor they knew what to do," she said. "I was walking along, waiting for death."

Finally, a police officer approached and ordered her to drop
her bag.

"I carried out the command and stepped away from this
terrible bag," she said.

The psychology of black widows

Alexei Zakharov, who heads Moscow's Research and Applied
Science Center and specializes in the psychology of extreme sit-
uations, has interviewed would-be black widows in Russian
custody and said many have reported having been drugged.
All, he said, demonstrated signs of mental trauma.

The fact that they often are literally widows is telling, he said, because of a sense that they have become a burden on their husbands' families.

"Sometimes these women are told: 'You've been a sinner all your life. Allah punished you by taking your husband. Now it's time to restore yourself by doing your duty.'"

Zakharov says he has seen evidence of brainwashing techniques, in which religious phrases in Arabic are recited repeatedly. "They're gathered in large auditoriums, and they repeat a combination of sounds whose meaning they have no idea of. At the same time, they're making very rhythmic body motions. That, in fact, is one of the simplest and most primitive entrancing technologies."

In [the Chechen capital] Grozny, whatever understanding exists of suicide bombers appears to be more instinctive than scientific.

"You must either feel terribly bad to want to kill yourself, and others in the bargain, or you must be a complete lunatic. And when you see everything that's happened around here, you know the number of lunatics has increased," said Zarema Sadulayeva, an activist with the group Save the Generation in Grozny, which works to promote the welfare of Chechen youths.

In a region where large numbers of men have either joined the rebels or fled the country to avoid arrest by the Russians, women have taken on new roles, many said.

They are the teachers trying to keep the schools open when there is no electricity. They are the mothers standing each Monday outside the Russian government headquarters, demanding to know what has happened to their missing sons. They are the stooped shoulders hauling buckets of water up shattered stairways to 10th-floor apartments.

And some of them are suicide bombers.

Organizations to Contact

The editors have compiled the following list of organizations concerned with the issues debated in this book. The descriptions are derived from materials provided by the organizations. All have publications or information available for interested readers. The list was compiled on the date of publication of the present volume; the information provided here may change. Be aware that many organizations take several weeks or longer to respond to inquiries, so allow as much time as possible.

The Brookings Institution
1775 Massachusetts Ave. NW, Washington, DC 20036
(202) 797-6000 • fax: (202) 797-6004
e-mail: brookinfo@brook.edu • Web site: www.brookings.org

The institution, founded in 1927, is a think tank that conducts research and education in foreign policy, economics, government, and the social sciences. In 2001 it began America's Response to Terrorism, a project that provides briefings and analysis to the public and which is featured on the center's Web site. Other publications include the quarterly *Brookings Review*, periodic *Policy Briefs*, and books including *Terrorism and U.S. Foreign Policy*.

Center for Strategic and International Studies (CSIS)
1800 K St. NW, Suite 400, Washington, DC 20006
(202) 887-0200 • fax: (202) 775-3199
Web site: www.csis.org

The center works to provide world leaders with strategic insights and policy options on current and emerging global issues. It publishes books including *To Prevail: An American Strategy for the Campaign Against Terrorism*; the *Washington Quarterly*, a journal on political, economic, and security issues; and other publications including reports that can be downloaded from its Web site.

Council on American-Islamic Relations (CAIR)
453 New Jersey Ave. SE, Washington, DC 20003
(202) 488-8787 • fax: (202) 488-0833
e-mail: cair@cair-net.org • Web site: www.cair-net.org

CAIR is a nonprofit membership organization that presents an Islamic perspective on public policy issues and challenges the misrepresentation of Islam and Muslims. It publishes the quarterly newsletter *Faith in Action* and other various publications on Muslims in the United States. Its Web site includes statements condemning both the September 11, 2001, attacks and discrimination against Muslims.

Department of Homeland Security (DHS)
Washington, DC 20528
Web site: www.dhs.gov

The Department of Homeland Security was created in direct response to the terrorist attacks of September 11, 2001. Many formerly disparate offices became united in a mission to prevent terrorist attacks on American soil, reduce the country's vulnerability to terrorism, and effectively respond to attacks that did occur. The Department of Homeland Security took branches formerly of the departments of treasury, justice, agriculture, energy, commerce, transportation, and defense under its extensive wing. Services from the coast guard to customs are now linked under the same umbrella, all with the singular mission of protecting the United States from attack.

Foundation for Middle East Peace
1763 N St. NW, Washington, DC 20036
(202) 835-3650 • fax: (202) 835-3651
e-mail: info@fmep.org • Web site: www.fmep.org

The foundation assists the peaceful resolution of the Israeli-Palestinian conflict by making financial grants available within the Arab and Jewish communities. It publishes the bimonthly *Report on Israeli Settlements in the Occupied Territories* and additional books and papers.

International Policy Institute of Counter-Terrorism (ICT)
PO Box 167, Herzlia 46150 Israel
972-9-9527277 • fax: 972-9-9513073
e-mail: mail@ict.org.il • Web site: www.ict.org.il

ICT is a research institute dedicated to developing public policy solutions to international terrorism. The ICT Web site is a comprehensive resource on terrorism and counterterrorism, featuring an extensive database on terrorist attacks and organizations, including al Qaeda.

Islamic Supreme Council of America (ISCA)
1400 Sixteenth St. NW, Room B112, Washington, DC 20036
(202) 939-3400 • fax: (202) 939-3410
e-mail: staff@islamicsupremecouncil.org
Web site: www.islamicsupremecouncil.org

The ISCA is a religious nongovernmental organization that promotes Islam in America both by integrating Islamic teachings with American culture and by teaching non-Muslims that Islam is a religion of moderation, peace, and tolerance. It strongly condemns Islamic extremists and all forms of terrorism. Its Web site includes statements, commentaries, and reports on terrorism, including *Osama bin Laden: A Legend Gone Wrong* and *Jihad: A Misunderstood Concept from Islam*.

Middle East Institute
1761 N St. NW, Washington, DC 20036-2882
(202) 785-1141 • fax: (202) 331-8861
e-mail: mideasti@mideasti.org
Web site: www.themiddleeastinstitute.org

The institute's charter mission is to promote better understanding of Middle Eastern cultures, languages, religions, and politics. It publishes numerous books, papers, audiotapes, and videos as well as the quarterly *Middle East Journal*. It also maintains an educational outreach department to give teachers and students of all grade levels advice on resources.

Middle East Media Research Institute (MEMRI)
PO Box 27837, Washington, DC 20038-7837
(202) 955-9070 • fax: (202) 955-9077
e-mail: memri@memri.org • Web site: www.memri.org

MEMRI translates and disseminates articles and commentaries from Middle East media sources and provides analysis on the political, ideological, intellectual, social, cultural, and religious trends in the region.

Middle East Policy Council (MEPC)
1730 M St. NW, Suite 512, Washington, DC 20036
(202) 296-6767 • fax: (202) 296-5791
e-mail: info@mepc.org • Web site: www.mepc.org

The purpose of this nonprofit organization is to contribute to an understanding of current issues in U.S. relations with countries of the Middle East. It publishes the quarterly journal *Middle East Policy* as well as special reports and books.

Middle East Research and Information Project (MERIP)
1500 Massachusetts Ave. NW, Suite 119, Washington, DC 20005
(202) 223-3677 • fax: (202) 223-3604
Web site: www.merip.org

MERIP's mission is to educate the public about the contemporary Middle East, with particular emphasis on U.S. policy, human rights, and social justice issues. It publishes the bimonthly *Middle East Report*.

U.S. Department of State, Counterterrorism Office
Office of Public Affairs, Room 2507
2201 C St. NW, Washington, DC 20520
(202) 647-4000
e-mail: secretary@state.gov • Web site: www.state.gov

The office works to develop and implement American counterterrorism strategy and to improve cooperation with foreign governments. Articles and speeches by government officials are available at its Web site.

Washington Institute for Near East Policy
1828 L St. NW, Washington, DC 20036
(202) 452-0650 • fax: (202) 223-5364
e-mail: info@washingtoninstitute.org
Web site: www.washingtoninstitute.org

The institute is an independent, nonprofit research organization that provides information and analysis on the Middle East and U.S. policy in the region. It publishes numerous books, periodic monographs, and reports on regional politics, security, and economics.

Bibliography

Books

Peter I. Bergen

Holy War, Inc.: Inside the Secret World of Osama bin Laden. New York: Free Press, 2002.

Joyce M. Davis

Martyrs: Innocence, Vengeance, and Despair in the Middle East. New York: Palgrave Macmillan, 2003.

John L. Esposito

Unholy War: Terror in the Name of Islam. New York: Oxford University Press, 2002.

Judith Palmer Harik

Hezbollah: The Changing Face of Terrorism. New York: I.B.Tauris, 2004.

Michael Ignatieff

The Lesser Evil: Political Ethics in an Age of Terror. Princeton, NJ: Princeton University Press, 2004.

Mark Juergensmeyer

Terror in the Mind of God: The Global Rise of Religious Violence. Berkeley: University of California Press, 2003.

Charles W. Kegley Jr.

The New Global Terrorism: Characteristics, Causes, Controls. Upper Saddle River, NJ: Prentice-Hall, 2002.

Bernard Lewis

The Crisis of Islam: Holy War and Unholy Terror. Waterville, ME: Thorndike Press, 2003.

Mahmood Mamdani

Good Muslim, Bad Muslim: America, the Cold War, and the Roots of Terror. New York: Pantheon, 2004.

Gus Martin

Understanding Terrorism: Challenges, Perspectives, and Issues. Thousand Oaks, CA: Sage, 2003.

Ahmed Rashid

Jihad: The Rise of Militant Islam in Central Asia. New York: Penguin Books, 2003.

Christoph Reuter

My Life Is a Weapon: A Modern History of Suicide Bombing. Princeton, NJ: Princeton University Press, 2004.

Marc Sageman

Understanding Terror Networks. Philadelphia: University of Pennsylvania Press, 2004.

Shaul Shai

The Shahids: Islam and Suicide Attacks. New Brunswick, NJ: Transaction, 2004.

Jessica Stern

Terror in the Name of God: Why Religious Militants Kill. New York: Ecco, 2003.

Periodicals

Scott Atran — "Genesis of Suicide Terrorism," *Science*, March 7, 2003.

Robert J. Barro — "The Myth That Poverty Breeds Terrorism," *BusinessWeek*, June 10, 2002.

Ed Blanche — "Cult of the Kamikaze," *Middle East*, May 2003.

Randy Borum — "Understanding the Terrorist Mind-Set," *FBI Law Enforcement Bulletin*, July 2003.

David Brooks — "The Culture of Martyrdom: How Suicide Bombing Became Not Just a Means but an End," *Atlantic Monthly*, June 2002.

Linda Butler — "Suicide Bombers: Dignity, Despair, and the Need for Hope: An Interview with Eyad El Sarraj," *Journal of Palestine Studies*, Summer 2002.

Marjorie Cohn — "Understanding, Responding to, and Preventing Terrorism," *Arab Studies Quarterly*, Spring/Summer 2002.

Christopher Dickey — "Inside Suicide, Inc.," *Newsweek*, April 15, 2002.

Carl N. Edwards — "The Mind of the Terrorist," *Forensic Examiner*, May/June 2003.

Robert Fisk — "What Drives a Bomber to Kill the Innocent Child?" *Independent*, August 11, 2001.

Helen Gibson — "'New Recruits' Why Did Two Quiet, Well-Liked Young British Men Travel to Israel to Become Suicide Bombers?" *Time International*, May 12, 2003.

Suzanne Goldenberg — "A Mission to Murder: Inside the Minds of the Suicide Bombers," *Guardian*, June 11, 2002.

Michael Gove — "Sympathy for Suicide Bombers Is a Sign of Moral Failure," *Times* (London), June 25, 2002.

Katie Grant — "Would You Die for Your Faith?" *Spectator*, November 10, 2001.

Sandra Jordan — "The Women Who Would Die for Allah," *New Statesman*, January 14, 2002.

John Kelsay — "Suicide Bombers: The 'Just War' Debate, Islamic Style," *Christian Century*, August 14, 2002.

Alan B. Krueger and Jitka Maleckova — "Does Poverty Cause Terrorism?" *New Republic*, June 24, 2002.

Gal Luft — "The Palestinian H-Bomb: Terror's Winning Strategy," *Foreign Affairs*, July/August 2002.

Thomas W. Murphy — "The Making of a Suicide Bomber," *USA in Review*, April 28, 2002.

Martha Brill Olcott and Bakhtiyar Babajanov	"The Terrorist Notebooks," *Foreign Policy*, March/April 2003.
Daniel Pipes	"God and Mammom: Does Poverty Cause Militant Islam?" *National Interest*, Winter 2001.
Ilene R. Prusher	"As Life Looks Bleaker, Suicide Bombers Get Younger," *Christian Science Monitor*, March 5, 2004.
Amanda Ripley	"Why Suicide Bombing Is Now All the Rage," *Time*, April 15, 2002.
Eyad Sarraj	"Why We Blow Ourselves Up," *Time*, April 8, 2002.
Daya Somasundaram	"Child Soldiers," *British Medical Journal*, May 25, 2002.
Ehud Sprinzak	"Rational Fanatics," *Foreign Policy*, September 2000.
Jessica Stern	"When Bombers Are Women," *Washington Post*, December 13, 2003.
Matthew Stevenson	"Suicide Soldiering: Through the Ages," *American Enterprise*, December 2001.
Quintan Wiktorowicz and John Kaltner	"Killing in the Name of Islam: Al-Qaeda's Justification for September 11," *Middle East Policy*, Summer 2003.
Fareed Zakaria	"Suicide Bombers Can Be Stopped," *Newsweek*, August 25, 2003.

Index

90